Stuck Stuck Stuck Stuck Stuck Stuck Stuck Stuck Stuck Stuck Stuck Stuck Stuck Stuck
Stuck Stuck Stuck Stuck Stuck Stuck Stuck Stuck Stuck Stuck Stuck Stuck Stuck Stuck
Stuck Stuck Stuck Stuck Stuck Stuck Stuck Stuck Stuck Stuck Stuck Stuck Stuck Stuck
Stuck Stuck Stuck Stuck Stuck Stuck Stuck Stuck Stuck Stuck Stuck Stuck Stuck Stuck
Stuck Stuck Stuck Stuck Stuck Stuck Stuck Stuck Stuck Stuck Stuck Stuck Stuck Stuck
Stuck Stuck Stuck Stuck Stuck Stuck Stuck Stuck Stuck Stuck Stuck Stuck Stuck
Stuck Stuck Stuck Stuck Stuck Stuck Stuck Stuck Stuck Stuck Stuck Stuck
Stuck Stuck Stuck Stuck Stuck Stuck Stuck Stuck Stuck Stuck Stuck
Stuck Stuck Stuck Stuck Stuck Stuck Stuck Stuck Stuck Stuck
Stuck Stuck Stuck Stuck Stuck Stuck Stuck Stuck Stuck
Stuck Stuck Stuck Stuck Stuck Stuck Stuck Stuck
Stuck Stuck Stuck Stuck Stuck Stuck Stuck
Stuck Stuck Stuck Stuck Stuck Stuck
Stuck Stuck Stuck Stuck Stuck Stuck
Stuck Stuck Stuck Stuck Stuck
Stuck Stuck Stuck Stuck
Stuck Stuck Stuck
Stuck Stuck
Stuck

Stuck

Asperger's Syndrome and Obsessive-Compulsive Behaviors

D1065615

Jonathan Hoffman, Ph.D., ABPP

Weston Press

Weston, Florida

A portion of the proceeds from the sale of this book
will be donated to charities for
Asperger's syndrome and obsessive-compulsive behaviors.

Weston Press, LLC
2233 N. Commerce Parkway
Suite 3
Weston, Florida 33326

ISBN: 978-0-9834549-4-6

*To all the children with Asperger's syndrome
and their dedicated parents, educators, and clinicians*

Bad habits are like a comfortable bed,
easy to get into, but hard to get out of.

—Anonymous

Act as if what you do makes a difference. It does.

—William James

Contents

Introduction

Life changes the moment a child is diagnosed with Asperger's syndrome. This is the case even if the parents, or others who are involved, have known in their hearts that something was different about the child before the words were uttered, that a more significant problem existed than mere quirkiness, sensitivity, or unusual habits or interests. After the child is identified with Asperger's, the biggest questions often include "What does this label really mean?" and "What can be done to help?"

The more they understand the complex nature of Asperger's syndrome—especially when it involves the presence of obsessive-compulsive behaviors that so often impede making progress—the more caregivers will have the potential to help in constructive ways. *Stuck* was written with this focus in mind, among others, including:

- Recognizing the importance of early diagnosis and treatment
- Increasing awareness of the many challenges that can be expected for children with Asperger's syndrome and their support team, especially their parents
- Understanding how obsessive-compulsive behaviors can affect the social and emotional growth of children with Asperger's, and what can help
- Providing strategies for helping the child cope with this difficult problem
- Strengthening the ability to communicate effectively with the affected child
- Finding professional help, when needed, and knowing what to look for
- Advocating effectively with health professionals, educators, friends, and relatives
- Stressing the importance of caregivers not neglecting their own needs, including anticipating and preparing for the challenges they and their children must face

For parents, indeed for all concerned with assisting children with Asperger's syndrome, the process of getting unstuck means something entirely different from eliminating or "fixing" the problem. It means being open-minded about developing different perspectives, as well as learning and practicing new skills even if they are uncomfortable at first. It also requires the ability to simultaneously be realistic and maintain a positive attitude through trying times; no easy task, of course.

Throughout this book, there are practical, action-oriented activities designed to increase awareness, reinforce learning, and support the development of effective intervention strategies. Helping a child with Asperger's syndrome make changes often means that those who care about the child will have to make some changes too, sometimes difficult ones. It is my hope that readers—whether parents seeking more in-depth information or educators and healthcare professionals looking for a resource about this topic for their own use or to share with others—will find *Stuck* beneficial in this process.

—Jonathan Hoffman

Section I
Understanding Asperger's Syndrome

Some will be reading this material with little or no background about this condition; others may be extraordinarily well versed. This section is intended to provide an overview of Asperger's syndrome.

Some History

Although the Austrian pediatrician Dr. Hans Asperger first described an autistic-like condition—he called it autistic psychopathy—with specific deficits in social comprehension and functioning in the 1940s,[1] it was only in the early 1980s that Dr. Lorna Wing, a psychiatrist, published her famous article that coined the term Asperger's syndrome.[2] Knowledge of the prevalence of Asperger's syndrome (AS) and the need for better diagnostic methods and more effective interventions became more widely known not too many years ago; it was not until 1994 that AS was recognized as a diagnosis by the American Psychiatric Association.[3]

Recently, the contributions of dedicated individuals—among them, psychologist Dr. Tony Attwood, whose writings have greatly increased awareness of AS;[4] educator Carol Gray, who developed the social-stories approach;[5] Professor Simon Baron-Cohen, who advanced an understanding of "theory of mind" deficits associated with autism;[6] Catherine Lord, Ph.D., and her colleagues, who developed improved diagnostic techniques like the Autism Diagnostic Observation Schedule (ADOS);[7] and Dr. Temple Grandin, an animal scientist and best-selling author who has AS herself[8]—have dramatically increased the general public's knowledge about this

11

formerly obscure condition. Characters who openly have or may be presumed to have AS appear on TV and in films. People with AS have even been dubbed with a colloquial nickname: Aspies.

This book is especially timely given a development that is taking place as it is being written. Influential leaders in behavioral health have proposed that the AS diagnosis be folded into a more general autism spectrum disorders (ASD) category,[9] one that will delineate a continuum of severity rather than a subtype and, by tightening criteria for inclusion, prevent ASDs from becoming a catchall diagnosis that both loses meaning and validity over time and funnels off vital resources from those most in need. Another reason for this proposed change is the diagnostically confusing overlap of AS with high-functioning autism or other pervasive developmental disorders. Looking on the bright side, however, the concepts presented in this book may also be helpful in understanding and treating those with these closely related conditions.

On the other hand, the term Asperger's syndrome has been acceptable to many, especially high-functioning adults, in a way that autism has not. Opponents of these proposed changes highlight all the work that has gone into creating awareness and making AS comprehensible to educators, legislators, health professionals, and the public. They assert that this acceptance has facilitated many getting needed help who would otherwise be likely to fall through the cracks. Some are skeptical about how much these changes are motivated by clinical versus financial interests. However, the biggest worry for some seems to be that many children presently diagnosed with AS—maybe their own child—will not fit under the new criteria for having an ASD and might be reclassified into another diagnosis that will not qualify them for necessary benefits or educational services and accommodations.[10]

Diagnostic Criteria for Asperger's Syndrome

The American Psychiatric Association publishes the Diagnostic and Statistical Manual of Mental Disorders (DSM),[11] the most widely used diagnostic criteria for psychological and developmental problems. Asperger's syndrome is characterized in the DSM by (1) problems in social interaction; (2) problems in communication; and (3) restricted, repetitive, and stereotyped patterns of behavior, interests, and activities. These symptoms must be apparent by the age of three, which can complicate making a formal diagnosis when early developmental histories are not available for reasons such as the death of a parent or the lack of access to records in some cases of adoption.

In the DSM, AS is found under the general heading of pervasive developmental disorders, which also includes autistic disorder (classic autism); childhood disintegrative disorder; Rett's disorder; and pervasive developmental disorder, not otherwise specified (which means that not all the criteria to diagnose autistic disorder or AS are present, or that autistic-like symptoms are manifested atypically). The names Asperger's syndrome and Asperger's disorder (as it appears in the DSM) are synonymous; the choice was made to use Asperger's syndrome throughout this book, sometimes just abbreviated as Asperger's or simply AS.

Unlike autistic disorder, under standard DSM diagnostic criteria, in AS there are no significant developmental delays in general adaptive behavior, overall intellectual level, or language. However, some experts question this; they believe that an early language delay per se should not necessarily rule out AS, as such delays do not seem to well predict later differences in functioning that are more relevant to differentiating autism and AS.[12] Another issue with the DSM parameters is that many individuals who fit the most important diagnostic criteria for AS are actually found to have delays and ongoing deficits in general adaptive functioning. As mentioned above, how the next version of the DSM will affect the concept of Asperger's syndrome remains to be seen.

The limitations of any diagnostic label are something that parents should always bear in mind. This is especially true for AS, which is a complex, highly heterogeneous condition, meaning that it intertwines with many other conditions and problems. While diagnoses are useful in many ways for making communication more effective and for developing intervention plans, they can never fully capture the sense of any one child. They are not useful if they are misconstrued as boundary markers for success. A child might not have all of the characteristics of the prototypical child with AS, but just enough of them to make the diagnosis the best fit.

Demographics

Autistic spectrum disorders (ASDs) appear to be far more common than anyone first suspected, and in danger of becoming an even more monumental social problem. Statistics about the prevalence of ASDs seem lately to be trending upward alarmingly and greatly exceed those of twenty or thirty years ago. Highlighting this apparently emerging epidemic, the Centers for Disease Control tracks statistics for what seems to be a steadily increasing prevalence of ASD diagnoses.[13] Why this is happening is not entirely clear. Several factors may be contributory to the inflating numbers;[14] for example, children who received other diagnoses may now be falling under a loosened definition of autism, or people who would not have sought services for their children in the past may now be doing so. Another possibility is that the modified criteria for ASDs and increase in social acceptability has resulted in the inclusion of children who may have been previously not diagnosed or identified with a different condition, such as learning disabilities or mental retardation.[15] A question has also been raised as to whether some parents and professionals might seek an ASD label even if it is not technically accurate, since this may help them access more services and accommodations.

There are some parents and researchers, however, who believe that these kinds of explanations do not really account for the increase. They believe that escalations in the prevalence of the autistic spectrum are quite genuine, and they are not satisfied with the accounts offered by the recognized medical and scientific organizations to date.

Also, available data is based primarily on samples from North America and Europe; not as much is known about Asperger's in the rest of the world, including developing countries. Nor, for that matter, have rates of AS among different racial and ethnic groups been studied sufficiently. However, the available information suggests that like autism, AS is likely to be found in all countries and throughout the socioeconomic pyramid.[16]

Because parameters for inclusion in this diagnosis vary, prevalence rates of AS reported in the scientific literature are inconsistent. Adding to the complexity, according to experts like Dr. Attwood,[17] some children initially diagnosed as autistic and who have made progress in their condition, possibly as a result of early intervention programs, may later be reclassified as having AS.

Asperger's is far more prevalent in boys than in girls.[18] The reason for this disproportionate prevalence in males, however, is still not well understood. One contributing factor might be that girls with AS can be harder to identify. Asperger's also seems to be more common in families that have histories of depression or bipolar disorder.[19]

Causes of Asperger's Syndrome

There has been a great deal of speculation and controversy regarding the cause of autism spectrum disorders. Theories over the years have examined the effects of various single and combined early childhood vaccinations (recently the evidence[20] for a direct connection between the MMR [mumps, measles, rubella] vaccine and autism was rejected by major medical authorities), mother's age and weight, in utero oxygen deprivation, high fevers/seizures in infancy, food toxicities, and the negative effects of many other environmental factors. There have even been studies showing that rates of ASDs are concentrated at higher levels in certain geographic regions in the U.S.[21] These often seem to be areas with a lot of high-technology jobs, where adults with ASDs or near-ASDs (known as shadow syndromes) are prone to congregate, intermarry, and be likely to pass on these genetics to their children. This supports Dr. Baron-Cohen's assortive-mating theory,[22] which speculates that very high-functioning individuals with ASDs, or ASD-type traits (like very math- or science-oriented brains) are tending

15

to marry one another more than in the past. Among other factors, the increased ability of persons with ASDs to achieve higher social status and earn good incomes have made them more desirable marriage partners than they were in past eras. However, another possibility is that ASDs might be found more in these areas because parents might migrate to the places where more services for their children are available.

By and large, however, some combination of genetic and/or neurobiological differences creating a vulnerability that may or may not be expressed, depending on a variety of environmental factors, appears to be the best thinking regarding the cause of Asperger's syndrome at the present time.[23] As an illustration of the complex interactions between nature and nurture, if you have a biological child who was already diagnosed with an ASD, it is more likely, but very far from certain, that your next child will have similar characteristics.[24] In any event, searching for an exact cause for all ASDs has not been all that fruitful, just as there has been no singular explanation, no magic bullet, that explains all the different kinds of cancer.

This should not be taken to mean that research into the causes of Asperger's is a waste of time. Actually, there are many thought-provoking findings and more seem to be on the way. For example, it has been suggested that the reason why children on the autism spectrum miss social cues and prefer "sameness" might relate to hormonal differences that make them more sensitive to discomfort in their own physical states.[25]

Specifically, the relationship of social and behavioral deficits found in ASDs and early dysregulation of the brain hormone oxytocin is currently being investigated. This is an area of research that might actually have the potential to be translated into a medical approach.[26] Luckily, today's children with AS are living in a time when research into genetics, biology, and behavior holds more promise than ever.

An interesting side note: It has been suggested that our society itself is becoming ever more "Aspergery," as dependence upon technology-based interaction—commonly referred to as social networking—seems to be reducing the need and capacity for live socialization. Many neurotypical children (i.e., those who do not have neurodevelopmental problems) apparently prefer electronic communications to speaking on the phone or making the effort to actually get together. It is ironic that some of those who might be more comfortable in the world of computers are actually the ones creating the devices that are redefining the nature of everyone else's social interactions.

Parents may or may not speculate about the reason why their child developed AS. Sometimes the ideas that parents have about the causes of AS result from a thorough investigation of the available research findings, but often they are based on random information in the media, conversations with friends or relatives, or the parents' own understandably complex feelings. The problem is that having an overly emotional or faulty theory about why a child has AS may lead to unwarranted anger at oneself or others and to distrust of professionals, and consequently may unnecessarily interfere with getting necessary help.

Most importantly, if parents are stuck on the notion of blaming themselves for their child's AS, getting past this as quickly as possible is highly recommended. The idea that parents are to blame for literally causing Asperger's has been shown to be a myth. However, this is not to say that parents cannot impede the progress of a child with AS by lack of appropriate response to the problem or by modeling negative or socially inappropriate behaviors themselves.

Action for Parents

As you read this book, examine your preconceptions about AS to determine if they are likely to be accurate or are based on erroneous information, myth, guilty feelings, or something else personal to your own experience.

Complexities of Identifying Asperger's Syndrome

Some day in the future, scientific and medical advances may make it possible not only to identify and categorize autism spectrum disorders just on the basis of genetic markers or brain scans but also to specify exactly how the condition will be manifested in a particular child. This, in fact, is the goal of scientific research like the Autism Phenome Project begun at the MIND Institute, University of California-Davis.[27] There might even be ways to correct these problems as soon as they are detected in a child, or in the genetic profile of the parents. This possibility will, of course, raise all sorts of complex ethical issues that are beyond the scope of this book.

Turning to the difficulties of identifying Asperger's syndrome at present: To start with, recall that AS is a heterogeneous condition, which means that it does not manifest itself in quite the same way for each child; in fact, that's far from the case. Some of these children are quiet and withdrawn, while others are quite the opposite: excessively talkative, hyperactive, and impulsive. Some can superficially appear neurotypical; their AS becomes apparent only when you get to know them better or have the opportunity to observe them over an extended time period. It is a myth that all children with Asperger's prefer to spend their free time by themselves; many crave friends but just don't know how to make and keep them. Additionally, although many do, not all children with Asperger's have across-the-board poor eye contact either; for some this is highly situational.

There may be certain types of AS, just as there are certain types of people. Roughly speaking, some children with AS are rule followers, more serious and introverted; some are "wild," highly distractible or oppositional-defiant; still others are the hyperlexic type, who seem like precocious young scientists, obsessed with words and numbers, constantly chattering about subjects that interest them, and often initially impressing the adults in their lives as potential geniuses. Psychologist Alan Sohn and special education teacher Cathy Grayson delineated possible subtypes including those that approximate rule followers, logic followers, the over-controlled, the highly anxious, the highly negative, the emotion-oriented, the angry/resistant, and those that combine both ADHD and OCD features.[28] Of course, many children with Asperger's

18

seem to defy being categorized as any specific type. In the final analysis, it may well turn out there are many biological pathways underlying the various forms that AS takes.

By definition, AS is present in early childhood, and far more children are apparently being identified during this period than was the case even a short time ago. Yet, for a variety of reasons noted just below, there are many who are not accurately identified until their teenage or adult years.[29] Asperger's can range from fairly mild to extremely severe, although the term *mild AS* is actually misleading; the diagnosis of AS is always a significant issue. Nevertheless, milder forms of AS are commonly overlooked or mistakenly conceptualized as "just immaturity" or as a "phase" that will almost magically disappear with increasing age.

In higher-functioning children, the diagnostic process may be delayed for a number of reasons:

- masking by high intelligence
- symptoms and problems that overlap with other conditions
- vacillations in functioning (i.e., isolated times when the child's behaviors seem fairly typical)
- special talents, strengths, or achievements
- lack of physical stigmata or obvious signs of developmental problems
- ability to function more typically in selected one-on-one situations
- parental denial, whether failure to perceive or accept that their child is "differently minded," or lack of readiness to seek professional opinions

Some of the other factors that can mask AS include shyness, nonclinical quirkiness, anxiety, and oppositional-defiance.

At the same time, social skills deficits, atypical behavior or affect, odd communications, lack of insight, and peculiar mannerisms can result in confusing AS with other psychological conditions—namely, thought disorder/schizophrenia, depression, or personality disorders. Categories like nonverbal learning disorder (also known as nonverbal learning disability) and semantic-pragmatic disorder (also known as pragmatic language impairment) both concern deficits in the comprehension and use of social language. Although in each of these conditions, problems in the social realm theoretically occur less severely than in AS, in practice the boundaries between them and AS can be quite fuzzy.[30]

Some children with AS may appear deceptively typical during their regular medical checkups. Also, their parents may be misperceived by some practitioners as overly anxious or too focused on their child's every little issue. Both of these potential problems can result in parents receiving inaccurate reassurances about their child's development. And, although the acumen of a child's educators, health professionals, or others in the child's environment can certainly be credited with identifying many children with AS early on, in the end, it often seems to be parents' concerns—the sense that something is just not right with their child—and their persistence and resourcefulness in getting answers that lead the way to obtaining the correct diagnosis as early as possible.

The main point here is that failure to identify AS, or getting caught up in non-essential diagnostic distinctions, resulting in late diagnosis or misdiagnosis can undoubtedly have serious negative consequences: inappropriate medications, misdirected psychological and educational plans/placements, and conflicts and frustrations between parent and child.

Action for Parents

If diagnosis of AS is not clear in your child's case, make a list of the concerning behaviors and address them with your health professionals. You could also seek a second opinion by a practitioner who specializes in the assessment and treatment of ASDs.

Psychological Testing

While there is no definitive single test for Asperger's syndrome, accurate diagnosis is supported by the use of appropriate psychological instruments. The Autism Diagnostic Interview-Revised,[31] the Social Responsiveness Scale,[32] and the Autism Diagnostic Observation Schedule[33] are some examples of well-regarded developmental assessment tools that assist in the diagnosis of AS.

In order to arrive at the most accurate diagnostic impression, it is imperative that any test battery to assess AS include measures of adaptive functioning, such as the Vineland Adaptive Behavior Scales-Second Edition[34] and the Adaptive Behavior Assessment System-Second Edition (ABAS-II).[35] Adaptive functioning refers to children's everyday living skills, the ways they are able to take care of their own needs at age-appropriate levels or not. Deficits in adaptive functioning are characteristic of children with AS, even those with high levels of intellectual ability.

Asperger's-specific instruments and observations are not meant to be used in a stand-alone fashion but as part of a comprehensive evaluation that includes examination of intellectual functioning, learning and memory processes, and academic achievement; this scope is essential to provide a meaningful context for interpreting the AS-specific instruments.

To some extent, the diagnosis of AS is related to the degree that parents can be forthcoming and accurate when answering questions regarding their child's early years. It is also of great help to the assessment process when parents are able and willing to provide photographs and/or videos from as far back in their child's life as possible. These visual records help in determining whether the child's condition was present from the beginning and therefore is predominantly developmental in nature as opposed to being the result of some later change, which is more common in conditions that are better explained by a psychiatric or medical diagnosis, or the result of environmental stressors.

Some parents, as well as some practitioners, may question the time and expense needed for comprehensive testing. The value is that well-considered and comprehensive psychoeducational testing is an essential tool in clarifying general intellectual level, relative strengths and weaknesses relating to higher cognitive functions and academic proficiency, processing problems (e.g., auditory or visual-perceptive deficits), working memory (the memory function that enables the short-term storage and manipulation of multiple, complex facts and priorities), and processing speed. The analysis of data from these psychological assessments can be invaluable in guiding the overall treatment and educational plan. It may also help to think of these tests, for a clinical team, as being somewhat analogous to diagnostic methods such as X-rays and MRIs that are often necessary for medical doctors to come to the right conclusion. As with any thorough diagnostic process, it is important for psychological examiners to obtain general health information. Having the results of screenings for speech and language problems, vision, and hearing, and ruling out any medical conditions that may be confused with AS are part of doing a psychological assessment properly.

Psychological evaluation has the most potential usefulness when (1) the correct assessment methods are used by qualified practitioners; (2) conclusions and recommendations follow directly from the data; and (3) the results are discussed in a meaningful way with the parents. Optimally, evaluation findings would be translated into practical recommendations that can be implemented in a timely and effective manner. Frustratingly, there are many times when this ideal is just not feasible. Nevertheless, the information gleaned from the evaluation may provide understandings about the child's functioning that were not previously clear to parents, educators, and clinicians (and sometimes the child). For instance, discovering that an auditory processing problem exists may change parents' thinking regarding whether their child is defiant or, instead, is genuinely having difficulty comprehending verbal instructions.

Action for Parents

To facilitate future assessments, treatment implementation, and ongoing tracking of progress, gather your child's previous evaluations and treatment

documentation and organize them in chronological order. Write down any questions that you believe further evaluation could help clarify. To facilitate addressing these concerns at future consultations, keep this list as part of the child's file.

Reactions to Receiving the Diagnosis of Asperger's Syndrome

Parents reading this book are asked to think back to when they initially learned that their child had Asperger's syndrome. Was it like a punch in the stomach, or did you feel ashamed or oddly detached? Were you surprised, or were you expecting what was said? Did you accept and adjust rapidly to the diagnosis, or have you still not really accepted it? Did you feel as if somehow you were to blame, or did you bitterly try to place the blame on someone else? Was your spouse on the same page as you, or were there conflicts? Did you actively seek information, or did you withdraw and hope it would all just go away or magically work out? Did worries about where to find the necessary help, or how to afford it, cross your mind (possibly along with guilt over being concerned with money)?

How did you feel about the practitioners who made the diagnosis? Were you grateful or resentful? Did you perceive them as supportive and empathetic? Too matter-of-fact and uncaring?

Of course, how parents initially react to their child's receiving a diagnosis of AS may not indicate how they will feel once they have had some time to digest this information. However, acknowledging and understanding the diagnosis as fully as possible can help them prepare better for later important decisions about the care recommended for their child. Since how we react to challenging life situations is sometimes more important than the nature of the situation itself, how parents think about and respond to their child having AS may likely be related to the services and social opportunities they will consider, not to mention the quality of life their child will experience at home. Similarly, parents' perceptions about the motivations and potential value of the treatment providers they encounter can also be anticipated to have many ramifications for their child's treatment plan and ultimate level of progress.

Action for Parents

Reflect on the following: What are your present feelings and thoughts about the diagnosis of AS? Is either embarrassment or fear preventing further investigation of any ongoing concerns?

Problems Associated with Asperger's Syndrome

AS is often associated with poor eating and sleep habits. It also can overlap with other psychological conditions—sometimes referred to as co-morbidities— that themselves are associated with various problems, and vice versa. This interaction snowballs both diagnostic and treatment complexity. The following sections discuss topics that can assist in understanding AS more completely.

Theory of Mind and Social Reciprocity

Trying to have a responsive conversation, let alone a relationship, with many children with Asperger's can seem as if you are trying to play catch with someone who just doesn't grasp the basic concept of the game. Some children with AS have learned to fake it, but as time goes by, their parents or peers may come to realize that "they just don't get it."

Children with AS are characteristically lacking in a true idea of the feelings, ideas, interest levels, conflicting obligations, or time constraints of the other participant(s) in their social environment; in other words, they do not appear to have empathy. For example, they may go on ad infinitum about the current weather statistics and ignore the typical signs, like a glazed faraway expression, that the other person isn't interested. Even if asked to stop or change the subject, they often just continue, not so much being oppositional or intentionally rude, but more because they appear to think that the key aspect of a dialogue is their own perception of what is relevant or interesting. They often don't really understand that other people have interests and concerns that are just as important to them as their own are. In short, they appear to be missing out on the salient social cues and appreciation of others' inner lives that allow the back-and-forth verbal and nonverbal communication flow that occurs in the normal course of neurotypical relationships.

The previous paragraph concerns two matters that are essential in understanding AS: deficits in establishing a theory of mind and problems in social reciprocity. These problems are, for many experts, the essence of AS.

The term *theory of mind* refers to the capacity to comprehend the mind-sets of others: their thoughts, feelings, and motivations. Difficulties establishing a theory of mind means that children with AS may be thought of, for all intents and purposes, as mind-blind. Returning to the metaphor of playing catch, imagine engaging in this activity with another person who has minimal, if any, idea that the game has started, that success means getting the ball to the other player effectively, that it is important to maintain the correct distance apart, that the ball should be thrown at a reasonable speed, and that looking at your partner so that you can pick up cues that he or she is about to throw to you or is ready for your throw is very important. A dysfunction in visuomotor brain cells (mirror neurons) is one theory why this problem occurs in AS.[36] Research about theory of mind is ongoing.

Expanding on this concept, those with AS might be also conceptualized as context-blind. Neurotypical people might lose their sense of their surroundings, responsibilities, values, and consequences if they are extremely angry or anxious. Those with AS might be especially prone to losing their sense of social context in a similar way if they are intensely interested in something or experiencing strong emotions or, conversely, become detached. However, this sort of problem might be the exception for a neurotypical individual, as opposed to one who has AS, for whom functioning in this way is the rule rather than the exception.

Social reciprocity refers to the ability to respond to another person in a manner that is congruent with what that person is doing, saying, or perceived as intending. For instance, if a person greets you, it is congruent to acknowledge the greeting, not unilaterally launch into a monologue about sports statistics or manga (Japanese comics). These youngsters may not know how to—or even perceive the need to—communicate their own feelings and thoughts in order to establish or maintain mutual social relationships, even when those relationships involve meeting their basic needs and wants.

Action for Parents
Take notice of the interactions you observe, or perhaps are told about, for signs of mind-blindness, or marked difficulty "playing ball" conversationally.

Social Functioning and Inflexibility

Given these issues regarding theory of mind and social reciprocity, it would only be surprising if Asperger's were not characterized by problems in social functioning. Actually, the entire realm of social behaviors presents significant issues for children with AS. Typical manifestations include problems in nonverbal social behaviors, such as poor eye contact and facial expressions that are mismatched with situations and expected feelings. Children with AS often have what has been called the "hundred-mile stare," which contributes to the perception that they are off in their own world. It is usually much more difficult for these children to establish same-age relationships, which is the truer measure of one's social abilities, than to get along with either adults or much younger children. Adults tend to be more tolerant, and younger children usually lack the awareness to detect social atypicality in the way that same-age peers do.

Many children with AS know incredible amounts of information about selected topics that they spew in a manner that does not suit whatever situation they are in; this "little professor" (a term coined by Dr. Hans Asperger) approach is not exactly the social presentation most typical children warm up to. Unfortunately, these are the children who are often shunted off to the side, considered by others to be "weirdos," "geeks," or worse. Not all "little professors" opine in an overly serious, pseudo-adult fashion; some sound like childish caricatures of eccentric mad scientists.

Making and keeping friends is an important developmental task for most children, but it usually does not come naturally for children with AS. As noted earlier, it is a myth that children with AS are not interested in having friends; many are, some aren't. The issue is that making friends for children with AS is like being asked to join in a new song-and-dance routine without the ability to hear any or most of the music, without full access to the lyrics, and being unaware of the choreography. Sounds pretty awkward, doesn't it? Well, this problem is precisely what many children with AS are up against when it comes to making friends. Playdates with other children who have AS is no panacea either, especially if the interests they focus on are not quite similar enough. For instance, a boy with AS who desperately wants and needs friends might fail to make a social connection with another boy with AS because the specific cartoons or the games they like are different, and neither can be flexible enough to agree that having a friend is more important than liking the exact same things. Way more than neurotypical children, children with AS are prone to leaving a social experience if they are not the center of attention or don't hear about a topic that is immediately relevant or useful to them. Also, many parents soon discover that providing their child with a prepared script for a particular social situation might initially help but is not transferable to the next socialization opportunity, even if it seems to be very similar. Children with AS simply do not do well at decoding the similarity between many of the situations they experience; conversely, they are very attuned to the small differences. Reading, and responding well socially requires holistic perceptions and intuitive actions rather than the linear thinking and delayed behaviors that are typical in AS.

One of the biggest problems that children with AS have socially—

and one that is very frustrating to their parents—is their inflexibility. Lacking the freedom to respond in variable ways to a given situation is also known as being stimulus bound. Anyone who has experiences with children with AS cannot help but note how rigidly they act and appear to think. Helping them try a new approach, even for something that is causing them distress and that they actually complain about, can be a herculean task; it's as if they are locked in on a mission that only they can see. As is part and parcel of autistic conditions, preserving sameness seems very compelling to these children; it's hard to be flexible when you don't ever want anything to change. Inflexibility, as would be expected, is associated with the obsessive-compulsive behaviors found among children with AS, a topic that will be discussed at length later on.

Literality

Children with Asperger's often have difficulty comprehending sarcasm or understanding how meaning is altered by the way certain words are emphasized. For example, depending on inflection, "see ya" could mean a friendly "see you later" or be a curt dismissal. Because of their difficulty grasping social experiences in their entirety, children with AS often become overreliant on "logic" to understand the social world, which most know does not operate on anything remotely resembling logic. Their basic problems in social abstraction may be reflected in difficulty interpreting unfamiliar idiomatic expressions and proverbs. Thus, a casual "talk to you later" may lead a child with AS to feel let down that the person didn't get back in touch that very day.

When a parent (or a clinician) asks a child with AS, "How are you?" the answer "I'm fine" often may not be responsive to the actual intent of the question and may mean that the child feels fine right then and there. In other words, children with AS are prone to failing to report an important life event or difficulty that they have recently experienced (e.g., conflict at home, getting bullied). It also doesn't help matters that many children with AS equate modifying the literal truth for the sake of social propriety to lying.

The problem depicted in this example is one of excessive literality. Being too literal, which relates to having difficulties following nuances of social communication, is common in AS. Literality means sticking to exact definitions rather than grasping underlying meanings. Another example of literality is a boy going down a slide headfirst after being instructed not to. The boy then points out that he did not disobey because he had his hands out in front of him when he went down the slide. Similarly, a girl with AS who is asked "Why aren't you listening to me?" might miss the full meaning of the question and think she is being challenged about the actual process of listening rather than about how she is behaving. Another example is a child who takes exception when an adult says, "It looks like you got up on the wrong side of the bed today." How would the adult know what side of the bed the child actually arose from?

Sometimes literality causes these children to "correct" statements made to them, to the consternation of their parents. For instance, if a parent asks, "How was your playdate?" the child might retort, "It wasn't a playdate; we just talked." In another example, a girl with AS is asked to rate how much she likes various foods, on a scale of one to ten. When asked, "What is grilled cheese?" she replies, "A sandwich," instead of giving a numerical rating. Or a frustrated boy banging his head against a door is told to stop doing that; he stops doing "that" by banging his head on a wall instead.

Literality underlies many instances (of course, not all) of perceived oppositional-defiant behavior in children with AS. They tend to focus on the letter of the law rather than the spirit. That is, they attend to the specific words rather than the abstract generalization. An illustration of this would be a child who appears to be oppositional because he texts a friend he has been asked not to call.

It's hardly surprising that some children with AS might actually threaten to "sue" their parents because minor promises, which they perceived, literally, as binding contracts, were violated. An example would be a parent who "promises" to bring back a Coke but instead gets a Pepsi because that is what the take-out restaurant has to offer and the child believes that this might constitute grounds for a lawsuit.

Action for Parents
Identify instances when literality interferes with your child's functioning with you. Try attending closely to how you react to such statements and whether or not your response is moving communication forward.

Speech and Language

Many parents experience a communication gap between themselves and their child with Asperger's in regard to their use of speech and language. Sometimes there is a huge gap, like talking to someone who seems to have come from another time and place. Sometimes it is more like the difference between American and British English—while it's the same basic language there are just enough differences to cause confusion and misunderstanding.

Children with AS often sound monotonic or speak with a peculiar inflection and syntax sometimes referred to as "Aspergerese." They might also have difficulties modulating the loudness of their voices, not understanding when different situations call for raising or lowering the volume. Some even sound a bit like Mr. Spock, the uber-logical Vulcan of *Star Trek* fame. They may use words in casual conversation that sound unusually stilted or archaic. For example, they may refer to a child they have socialized with as their counterpart rather than their friend. Some may speak in a way that others could mistakenly take as an indication that they are not speaking their native language. Of course, it is possible that a child with AS does not have this unusual way of speaking.

Self-Centeredness and Emotional Sensitivity

It's discouraging, but children with Asperger's may act as if they do not return the love and care their parents provide. They also often appear very self-centered and seemingly function as if there are no other perspectives or needs than their own, even when in the midst of a warm and secure family. It is imperative that parents of children with AS understand that this is not intentional, it's just part of the condition.

The effect this self-centeredness has on making and sustaining friendships is quite problematic, especially as they get older and the need to show at least a modicum of interest and care for one's friends is necessary. Paradoxically, children with AS can show high degrees of awareness and caring regarding animals, people who are physically ill or disabled, and social problems like poverty. Transferring this same level of social sensitivity into viable levels of social understanding in their interactions with same-age peers and family members is one of the great challenges of treatment efforts. It is all too easy for parents to misinterpret their child's ability to be sensitive in the abstract as indicating a higher level of social comprehension than the child actually has.

Action for Parents
Separate your child from their condition by not judging how they might appear self-centered or insensitive in the same way as you would a neurotypical child.

Restricted Interests

Atypical or restricted interests are characteristic of many children with Asperger's. For example, they may want to learn about and/or talk about only one topic—like maps, sports, weather events, unusual statistics, movies, computers, video games, dinosaurs, historical dates, military facts, mechanical functions, animals, superheroes, or a particular card game—to the exclusion of other interests. At first, some parents may be enthralled by their youngster's attainment of factual information, particularly if they happen to share similar interests or out of sheer love have decided they must partake in their

child's world, no matter how fantastical. However, as time goes on, most come to sadly realize that the preoccupation with accumulating piecemeal knowledge is actually atypical and indeed detrimental to their child's social and emotional development.

Children with AS may hold one intense interest to the exclusion of all others or have a series of special interests that may change as they get older. Some children have multiple interests that are all intense but not equally so at a given time. An atypical but compelling interest (also known as a fixation) or a very isolated, highly developed but ultimately purposeless ability (known as a splinter skill, or in the extreme form, a savant skill, like a boy's instantaneously being able to play a song on the piano that he's heard only one time even though he has never had lessons) is, at times, hard to distinguish from a truly viable talent or passion that might one day lead to vocational success. For instance, it is not unheard of that a child's preoccupation with computers later leads to a job or even an unusual level of success in technology, but this is not the usual case. Even if a child with AS has a genuinely useful talent, without the commensurate social abilities, the chances of being able to capitalize on it are likely quite slim.

Unfortunately, many parents can be misled by false hopes for years, and fail to help their child explore more realistic options and develop the vocational and social skills needed to truly succeed in the workplace. For example, since many of those with AS are fond of memorizing movie dialogue or become preoccupied with film trivia, their parents erroneously believe that a career in the cinema, like becoming a director, is a viable opportunity. It can be a shattering experience for parents when it becomes clear by their child's late adolescence or early adulthood that for the vast majority this dream is a fantasy. (Of course, this happens when a child is neurotypical too but the potential consequences are probably much less drastic.) Preoccupations and restrictions of interests may become so pronounced that they are appropriately categorized as obsessive-compulsive behaviors.

Sensorimotor Functioning

Parents of children who are eventually diagnosed with Asperger's and obsessive-compulsive behaviors often retrospectively describe sensorimotor issues as being one of the first signs that there might be a problem in their child's development.

Some children with AS are physically awkward, which often reflects fine and/or gross motor problems. They may not respond to the weather being cold or hot in typical ways; for example, a child with AS may insist on wearing a warm jacket on sweltering summer days, or shorts on a cold one. Additionally, they are often highly sensitive to certain noises, like ticking clocks or buzzers or bells, and might be prone to putting their hands over their ears in public settings that are loud, like movie theaters or restaurants. Sometimes these children chew on their clothing or stretch their shirts out to feel looser. They can also show pronounced aversions to certain smells or, conversely, become preoccupied by smelling various objects or their own hands, skin pickings, or mucus.

Children with AS can experience difficulties in coordinating facial muscles in a way that properly conveys their emotional state. They are often very selective about foods due to texture or taste concerns (e.g., they will restrict their eating to a few foods like pasta and cereal that they can tolerate, or have idiosyncratic eating habits that might, in part, relate to coordination problems (e.g., they will not use utensils, or they get their food all over their faces without realizing they need to use napkins). This latter group of issues can lead to problems in

33

getting adequate nutrition, as well as limiting participation in physical exercise and sports. Sensorimotor problems, which are likely to relate to sensorimotor obsessions or compulsions, often explain why many children with AS prefer indoor to outdoor play: They are less exposed to discomforting stimuli. Unfortunately, insufficient nutrition and lack of exercise that stem from sensorimotor problems often affect the ability of children with AS to concentrate and learn as well as possible, which leads into the subject of the next section.

Problems in Attention, Concentration, and Impulse Control

Problems in attention and concentration as well as impulsivities can accompany Asperger's in many children. Therefore, it is not surprising that features of attention-deficit (hyperactivity) disorder (ADHD) are frequently present in this population. ADHD is often thought to reflect a basic difficulty in "executive functioning."[37] Executive functioning refers to the capacity to plan and organize information in a relevant and useful manner. Those with ADHD are also thought to have particular problems regarding their self-instructional skills. That is, they may have difficulty reflecting and talking themselves through complex or stressful challenges. While the DSM does not allow for the formal diagnosis of ADHD when a pervasive developmental disorder like AS is diagnosed,[38] it nevertheless seems helpful to convey some information about this clinical entity.

In the DSM at present, the subtypes of ADHD are inattentive type, hyperactive/impulsive type, combined type, and ADHD not otherwise specified (NOS), which is diagnosed when the necessary criteria for the other types are not met. Some of the signs of ADHD are:

- distractibility, particularly on nonpreferred tasks
- perseverating on preferred tasks or interests
- poor organizational skills
- losing or misplacing needed items

- appearing to be daydreaming
- difficulty sitting still, being fidgety
- impulsivity (e.g., calling out in class)

It sounds counterintuitive, yet often perfectionism and other obsessive-compulsive characteristics are part of the ADHD profile; a particular individual can manifest both ADHD and obsessive-compulsive behaviors, and even outright obsessive-compulsive disorder. This appears due to the fact that some brains can variably, often unpredictably, be prone to the extremes of "too stuck and too loose" as a function of a variety of complex biological and situational factors.

Problems in Thought Process and Perception

Recently, there has been recognition that some children with Asperger's are at risk for developing serious disorders of thought and perception as they approach adulthood.[39] In the most worrisome cases, the child may appear delusional or paranoid. In other words, they may start to have trouble distinguishing reality from fantasy. As an example referencing obsessive-compulsive behaviors, a boy who is compulsive about the location of his possessions, noticing an inevitable minor positional variation might, over time, start to irrationally accuse his parents of moving his items on purpose. This possibility again underscores the need for prompt and sufficient levels of intervention. For those with AS, early identification and treatment can potentially lessen risk factors for developing major psychiatric problems.

Action for Parents

Even though parents usually know their child best, if uncharacteristically peculiar thoughts or behaviors arise, don't delay in contacting your health professionals.

Anxiety, Depression, Poor Self-Image, and Irritability

Negative emotional states—like anxiety, depression, poor self-image, and being easily irritated—are frequently present in a child with Asperger's syndrome, but may tend to be minimized or under-addressed because they are often overshadowed by the compelling nature of other problems the child manifests. However, when the child's emotional distress or reactivity is very overwhelming or expressed with self-defeating or avoidance behaviors, attempts at making positive changes can easily become derailed. On the other hand, in a certain respect, experiencing some degree of distress may show a level of self-awareness that has potential for being shaped constructively; it is likely that the children with AS who are the most indifferent to their circumstances will ultimately be the hardest to help.

In the category of anxiety disorders (other than obsessive-compulsive disorder, which will be the focus of subsequent sections of this book) children with AS can manifest generalized anxiety disorder, specific phobia, social phobia (social anxiety disorder), or panic disorder as coexisting conditions.

Persistently high levels of anxiety and muscle tension that appear to be present regardless of the particular situation that a child is experiencing might reflect generalized anxiety disorder. A specific phobia is indicated when anxiety escalates to unrealistic proportions when the child is confronted by a dog, bugs, an elevator, or some other circumscribed trigger, and the child actively tries to avoid further exposure to these stimuli. When the child's anxiety centers on a debilitating, excessive fear of becoming embarrassed in certain social settings or in situations that call for publicly performing in some way, like giving a class presentation or eating in the lunchroom, a concomitant social phobia may exist. Highly anxious children with AS may be even more prone than they would be otherwise to develop a specific phobia about attending school. The diagnosis of panic disorder requires more than just the experience of panic attacks, which are sudden, often unexpected episodes of intense fear that peak in no more than ten minutes. They can include a number of discomforting symptoms, including heart racing (palpitations), nausea, feeling very detached from oneself (depersonalization) or reality (derealization), shortness of breath, dizziness, sweating, body sensations like tingling or numbness (paresthesias), and fear of losing control or one's mind. To reach diagnostic criteria for panic disorder, children must also show fear of having further attacks (anticipatory anxiety) and manifest avoidance of situations that might trigger attacks or use compensatory "safety signals" to ward off attacks, like staying aware of the closest exit in a public building. The most severe form of avoidance related to panic disorder is called agoraphobia, which can get so bad that people virtually become prisoners in their own homes, afraid that venturing out of their comfort zones will set off severe bursts of anxiety.

It's important for parents to avoid jumping to conclusions about the reasons for any particular anxious behavior that their child is demonstrating. Insisting on sitting in a certain seat could reflect an obsessive-compulsive behavior, a panic disorder, or—and sometimes this can get confusing—the interaction of both. Likewise, refusing to participate on a sports team could indicate a lack of interest in having the social interaction itself, anxiety about making a bad play in front of peers and onlookers, or fear that bugs will be around.

Having trouble decoding the social world while at the same time being at least somewhat aware that they are "different" is a dual issue often faced by children with AS. This problem is heightened if they are being teased or physically bullied, or are being excluded through overt rejection or by being treated as if they are invisible. This awareness may reach an apex during adolescence and result in feelings of sadness, negativism or, worse, in clinical levels of depression. A child with AS may be experiencing clinical depression if significant levels of sadness have lasted two weeks or more and are accompanied by severe withdrawal, crying episodes, increased comments indicating helplessness and hopelessness, sleeping too much, and notable alterations in eating habits. In younger people, depression may be masked and expressed as boredom. Identifying depression in children with AS is complicated by their inherent difficulties in emotional awareness and communication. Asperger's or not, suicidal thoughts and actions are associated with depressive feelings. Children with AS who are expressing suicidal ideation, especially if a specific plan or time is indicated, need immediate assessment of their safety. It is a myth that those who talk about suicide never do it. Parents need to increase their observations if they start hearing more comments from their child questioning why he or she was born, what the purpose of life is, or how everyone would be better off if the child were not around. Can children with AS use threats of committing suicide to manipulate their parents? Definitely; nonetheless, this is a time when seeking the advice of a mental health professional is absolutely necessary. Suicidal threats need to be thoughtfully addressed, as the very act of threatening to hurt oneself is a serious matter.

A common aspect of depression among those with AS is a negative self-image; this can be a problem even when children have experienced a great deal of love and acceptance from their families. Unfortunately, this problem may actually be worse among those children who are relatively the most self-aware. Being highly self-critical, particularly about their intelligence and/or appearance, is a common sign of poor self-image, just as it is for neurotypicals.

Some children with AS are very even-tempered; some have periods of heightened irritability; some are irritable almost all the time. Irritability may be observed as constant complaining, whining, fussiness, or being easily annoyed, as well as more dramatically in angry outbursts or highly oppositional behaviors. Irritability compounds social issues by making the child unpleasant to be around. In some cases, irritability may be another sign of underlying depression. In others, it may be a result of stress or reflect an intrinsic, unhelpful aspect of the child's personality. Children with Asperger's can be aggressive as well—explosive outbursts, even seriously violent behaviors, are, unfortunately, an all too common problem in this population. Aggression among those with AS seems to peak in the earlier years of age and appears to be most present in those who are particularly resistant to making changes and are prone to having more ritualistic behaviors. Boys and girls with AS do not appear to be all that different regarding their potential for aggression.[40]

Action for Parents

Take any suicidal statements or violent threats seriously and take protective steps. Allow a professional to determine if the child "means it or not." Again, it is a myth that individuals who talk about suicide or hurting others never do it.

Difficulty Making Connections with Larger Purposes

Since Asperger's is characterized by focusing on the trees—perhaps even certain kinds of leaves—rather than on the forest, it may be difficult for those with this condition to transcend their limited focus, especially in reference to the exaggerated value they often attach to obtaining factual knowledge. For them, attaining the abstract ability to perceive higher purposes of being than what they are literally experiencing through their senses is very problematic. The upside of this is that they may be protected from the existential angst that troubles many with questions like "What is the meaning of life; why am I here?" On the other hand, the abiding comfort that many find through meaningful relationships and deep spiritual or religious engagement may not be truly available for many with AS.

The experience of two children, one with AS and the other neuro-typical, studying for a science test may look the same on the surface, but in reality may be quite different. The neurotypical child is far more like-ly to have the capacity to achieve a joy of learning beyond just attaining more facts or adhering to a parent's wishes by doing schoolwork. This brings up one of the most troubling aspects of AS, especially for parents: Is it possible for children to go beyond the material aspects of existence and find intrinsic satisfaction—enjoying life-enriching experiences like beauty and art for their own sakes, finding genuine self-actualization through work, or developing truly deep friendships and love? Addressing this issue is one of most daunting yet meaningful goals of clinical intervention; succeeding in it may well indicate that the best outcome possible for a child with AS has been achieved.

The Cyber World

Why do so many children with Asperger's seem to gravitate toward and even excel at computer and video games?[41] With the advent of smartphones, they often are intent on getting the latest version of them, particularly so they can keep up with all the new apps.

These high-tech activities favor those with logical minds that can narrowly and intensely focus in constricted fields for long periods of time. In addition, this world can exist entirely out of the social realm, allowing access to quasi-social interaction in which children do not have to contend with facial expressions or other kinds of nonverbal communication. The virtual world is very often accepting and nonjudgmental, and is easily escaped when it is not. Another aspect is that children with AS can practice the basic motor skills needed to advance in the computer and video world at their own pace and without the stress of being observed, especially when they make mistakes.

The cyber world provides many with AS a heightened, albeit illusory, sense of being in control. In this world, people are usually totally anonymous, so that social awkwardness or other signs of AS can be more easily disguised. Also, they can't be actually seen (unless they allow teleconferencing), a factor that many with AS prefer. And again, importantly, they can escape from any stress that they experience there very easily, just by switching to another site or turning off whatever they are doing. This sense of security in the virtual world is, of course, false and can lead those with AS to underestimate just how vulnerable they truly are.

Lately, there seems to be an emerging industry geared at creating cyber games and apps for those with AS. Some devise visual schedules to better organize the child's day, others provide virtual social skills practice.

The jury is still out as to whether children with AS can generalize social skills learned in a virtual format to real life any more than a child who only plays a video tennis game would be expected to be able to serve and volley in a regular match.

Many parents accept or even encourage their child's extensive computer and gaming involvement. They may believe that it would be cruel to prevent or even limit their isolated child from doing something he or she seems to enjoy. Or they may harbor hopes, usually overly optimistic, that this activity will lead their child to some kind of social acceptance or toward a lucrative career.

In sum, extreme involvement in the cyber world can present just another obstacle to a child's social development and can add what is known as a process addiction to the child's list of problems. This is a problem that has many similarities to other kinds of addictions, but without the more tangible aspect of taking an actual substance. It seems worth noting that some experts think there might eventually be sufficient research to justify Internet addiction as a specific diagnosis.

Action for Parents

Assess how much time your child is engaging in use of electronics and make sure that you truly know what they are accessing.

The Inner Experience of Having Asperger's Syndrome

Is it true that no matter how empathetic or knowledgeable parents may be, it is not possible to truly experience what Asperger's syndrome is like for their child any more than a sighted person can really know what it is like to be blind? Perhaps. However, not to diminish the qualitative and life-altering differences found among those with AS, it seems worth noting that many neurotypical people can identify times when they were at least a bit "Aspergery" themselves. For instance, most of us can relate to the experience of being too literal or, in hindsight, having been too rigid.

41

We also might easily identify with having been so stressed at some time that our awareness and concern about what other people around us were thinking and feeling became narrowly constricted, as if we were transiently mind-blind. Acknowledging this commonality can convey more insight into how children with AS might experience life.

In general, one imagines that out of their narrow safety zones, children with AS often feel uncomfortable in their own skins, as well as confused in environments that are not familiar, not under their control, or easy to ignore or escape. And it's no wonder—for the child with AS, experiencing life may be akin to watching a movie that is missing scenes or has dialogue that is randomly muffled or accentuated, or being asked to play very complex sheet music on a piano that is out of tune and simultaneously being exposed to unwanted, bothersome sensory input: aversive smells, unpleasant textures, and discordant sounds. Why should they want to interact with such a world?

While some with AS do not have sufficient ability (or perhaps interest) to communicate their internal experiences in a way that is comprehensible to listeners, others do. This may be done verbally or nonverbally through writing, art, or expressive movement, such as dance. In and of itself, it seems that learning to objectify one's inner life and share it with others would be therapeutically beneficial for those with AS. Also, people who can think about their own thought processes and emotions more objectively develop a means of comparing their internal experiences to those of others, thereby creating the potential for deeper levels of interpersonal connectivity and increased ability to attain more theory of mind, an important goal for children with AS.

An individual with Asperger's who had developed his ability to share his perspective about having AS put it this way (he is an animal lover, like many with AS): "I think I have more in common with how a dog thinks than [with] people who don't have Asperger's. I just see and think about what's right in front of me." Therapists often emphasize that living in the here and now is preferable; for those with AS, however, this way of living appears so exaggerated that it creates maladaptive social tunnel vision.

Action for Parents
Try not only accepting but also actively encouraging open discussions about Asperger's.

Gender and Asperger's Syndrome

Remember, boys greatly outnumber girls among children with Asperger's syndrome.[42] Boys and girls may also experience having AS in different ways, as a result of gender roles and other social expectations and norms, according to Dr. Tony Attwood's writings.[43] Asperger's in young girls may be harder to detect than in boys, particularly when the child is high functioning. These girls may find it easier than boys to remain on the fringes of social groups and mimic gender-expected social behaviors. Even parents might not readily recognize the existence of problems in true social comprehension if their daughter has a caring and sensitive nature.

A "little professor" girl may merely be considered brainy or serious, whereas a similar type of boy may be typed as weird and nerdy, or lacking masculinity. They may also tend to elicit bullying less than do boys, as sensitivity and eccentricity is more likely to correlate with male patterns of bullying behavior. Further, particularly at young ages, the status of a socially adept girl is more likely to be enhanced by befriending and shielding a socially atypical girl than is the case regarding a male of high social status doing the same.

Girls who find the complex social cues for girl groups hard to decipher may gravitate to the less socially nuanced male groups and be at least marginally socially acceptable; boys who cannot cope with the aggressiveness and raw taunting more typical of male groups cannot as easily turn to the females without drawing adverse attention, even mockery. When girls have restricted interests, this may be disguised by the fact that their interests tend to be closer to gender expectancies than those of boys with AS. For example, a boy may become obsessed with maps, a preoccupation that appears unusual across the board, whereas a girl may get preoccupied with a particular kind of doll that other girls

43

like; she will just get more intensely involved. Similarly, because of the interest in sports and other physical activities that is common among young males, a boy with AS might find it harder to hide his physical awkwardness than would a girl with AS among girls who are not as monolithically interested in these kinds of pursuits.

A sizable percentage of girls with anorexia nervosa may have AS that is masked by their eating disorder.[44] Depression, which is much more common among females, may also contribute to the failure to recognize that a girl has AS.[45]

Strengths

Having Asperger's syndrome hardly means a child does not have strengths. In fact, children with AS often have numerous strong points. Some of these children can be extremely creative and think innovatively, while others often notice details that pass by neurotypical children. Some excel at math and science. At times, even a normally aloof child can show surprising tenderness and affection. Some parents may despair of finding any strengths or positive attributes in their child. Look closer! Every single child with AS has special strengths that need to be recognized and cherished, even if they would seem inconsequential to others.

Dr. Martin Seligman has advanced an emerging field of positive psychology, in which enhancing strengths rather than focusing on deficits is paramount.[46] This approach seems highly applicable to AS. By focusing on developing their positive attributes, children with AS might discover avenues for personal growth and happiness that might be otherwise overlooked.

Action for Parents

Focus on identifying and encouraging your child's strengths as often as possible.

Very High Achievers with Asperger's Syndrome

In addition to variations in general level of adaptive functioning, there can be a wide range of intellectual levels and learning abilities and disabilities among children with Asperger's syndrome. In the pervasive developmental disorders category, individuals with more intact intellectual (IQ > 70) and learning abilities are called high functioning.

Intellectual proficiency and AS are hardly mutually exclusive. To the contrary, many children with AS are gifted and talented. Although no one can be really sure, there has been some lively speculation about famous individuals who seemed to present symptoms and problems reminiscent of AS. In *Asperger's Syndrome and High Achievement: Some Very Remarkable People*,[47] notables such as Michelangelo Buonarroti, Thomas Jefferson, and Albert Einstein are mentioned as possibly having Asperger's. Bram Cohen, a founder of BitTorrent, an influential high-tech company, publicly diagnosed himself as having AS. *The Big Short*, a bestseller, featured the story of Dr. Michael Burry, a medical school graduate turned brilliant investment manager who discovered he had AS well into adulthood.[48] James Durbin, a contestant on the popular TV show *American Idol*, revealed he has Asperger's syndrome too. It is likely that a lot of successful people in your community have Asperger's (consider some of the doctors, lawyers, high-tech professionals, and educators you have met).

Despite their extensive knowledge about particular subjects, even very intellectually advanced individuals with AS typically struggle to relate to the larger world. As noted earlier, their zeal for what interests them usually vastly exceeds the interest level of their audience, a fact that often tends to elude them. Yet, when one of these children's gifts for learning about a specific subject area matches an actual commercial, scientific, or academic need, and they develop adequate social skills, watch out! People with AS may be found among the highest achievers on earth when it comes to professional or financial success. The question is: Does this worldly success actually translate to a happy and well-integrated life?

Family Issues

Like all children, those with Asperger's syndrome do not exist in a vacuum, and their families are usually the most important aspect of their environment. Children with AS affect their families, just as families—with all their strengths and challenges—inevitably affect the adjustment and progress of children with AS. The ripple effect of having a child with AS is the proverbial stone thrown into a body of water: the water, in this instance, being the child's family.

Parenting Children with Asperger's Syndrome

Having a child with Asperger's is certainly not what most parents expect. Learning that your child has even the possibility of a condition that is discussed in the same breath as autism is naturally anxiety provoking, to say the least. As noted earlier, with any serious diagnosis, there is enormous variability in the way parents may respond at first. And if the diagnosis has been delayed, parents may become desensitized to atypical behaviors that would cause enormous consternation in most families. In other words, to them, an unusual way of functioning has become just ordinary, everyday life. It is often only when other adults or professionals become involved that these parents can see the true extent of their child's deficits.

For parents, even those most generally insightful and knowledge-able about AS, both the inability to comprehend or feel connected to their child and the realization that they are not truly understood by their child can be overwhelming and lead to a whole gamut of difficult emotions. Imagine the feelings of a father who is being treated for a brain tumor when his son with AS focuses only on the fact that his dad cannot drive him to his favorite comic book store.

Many parents of children with AS feel as if they are lost or incompetent, that they exist in a parallel parenting universe that has little reference point to "normal" parenting. Mostly, however, parenting children with AS is the same as parenting any other children—you love them, teach them, try to guide and protect them, and attempt to support them in attaining their goals. You soothe them when they are hurt or sick. You develop your own special relationship and try to make up quickly when the inevitable arguments and conflicts occur. The difference is that children with Asperger's need their parents' attention, understanding, and wisdom more. Therefore, creating an accepting, calm and nonjudgmental family atmosphere is essential. Sounds straightforward, doesn't it?

While some children with Asperger's syndrome are quite affectionate toward their parents, many have difficulty returning the love they receive in obvious ways. This lack of reciprocity can be very troubling to their parents, who are often facing many challenges to provide their child with a warm and loving home. While it's only natural for parents to hope for even small recognitions of their efforts—or absent such recognition, to experience a sense of rejection or hurt—it is important for parents to resist the temptation to let such feelings overtly affect their behavior toward their child. Even if they never really seem to show it, children with AS will likely do better in an atmosphere of love and affection, just like anybody else.

Social deficits associated with AS can inadvertently (and perhaps at times not so accidentally) place parents in unexpected, awkward, or outright embarrassing situations. For example, when introduced to someone new, children with AS might blurt out inappropriate comments or questions regarding that person's weight, race, or religion. Developing a high level of forbearance, a flexible point of view, and tolerance is doubtless very useful to these parents. So is a healthy sense of humor and of the absurd. It is also helpful for a parent to be prepared for socially awkward situations in advance. It's challenging for parents to know what to say to defuse a problem situation, as well as when it would be better not to come to the "rescue," for therapeutic reasons.

Asperger's syndrome must be taken into consideration in regard to setting expectations and giving consequences for undesirable behaviors. At the same time, however, it is no excuse for poor behavior. Like any other child, those with AS must be held accountable and receive appropriate discipline to learn to adhere to proper boundaries and conduct themselves in a responsible manner throughout their lives.

Also, as with any other child, teaching desirable social behaviors is more effectively accomplished using positive reinforcement, in the form of rewards, rather than punishment. Reinforcement works by associating behaving in a positive manner with earning tangible consequences, like a new toy or, even better, praise from a desired source of acknowledgment. For the most part, it is preferable to simply ignore nonaggressive or relatively minor infractions and, instead, concentrate on the process of helping the child make more constructive choices. Of course, it is important for parents not to confuse ignoring an undesirable behavior with acting negligently toward their child's true needs or not showing love.

Punishment often fails because it does not teach, it merely temporarily suppresses negative behaviors, and then usually only in the presence of a feared punisher. Also, a possible side effect of punishment is often resentment toward the punisher. Punishment is often confused with negative reinforcement; the former's objective is to reduce an unwanted behavior, while the latter strengthens a behavior by removing something negative. Like punishment, negative reinforcement can backfire. An example of a problem caused by negative reinforcement in parenting is picking up crying children to get them to stop. It might "work" but usually will result in more instances of their crying for attention in the future.

For major behavioral issues in younger children that cannot be ignored, such as physical aggression, true safety issues, and purposeful destruction of family property, time-out will usually suffice. Time-out technically means removal from the chance to receive positive reinforcement. The child must stay quiet and separate for a brief period; a commonly used rule of thumb is generally one minute per year of age. Upon successful completion of the time-out period, the child is allowed to resume normal activities. Until time-out is completed, reinforcements such as attention or access to desired activities or playthings are withheld. Inappropriately isolating children for long periods of time to teach them a lesson should not be misconstrued as time-out.

Although obtaining a high degree of factual knowledge about AS may be helpful, it is also important to realize that there is no "cookbook" approach to parenting a child with Asperger's any more than there is with a neurotypical child. The more relevant achievement is having an intervention plan that is grounded in good values, in addition to at least a basic understanding of the principles of parenting in a positive way.

Parents of children with AS often feel like they are facing an uncertain future. This concern isn't helped by the fact that no specialist can definitively state an exact prognosis for any individual child. Many parents come to find that keeping their focus on effective actions and reality-based planning in the present is more useful than remaining mired in past expectations about how life should have gone or wasting time and energy on unproductive worries about the future.

More discussion about parenting issues will take place in a later section of this book.

Action for Parents
Reflect on the aspects of parenting a child with AS that provide you with the most satisfaction.

Sibling Reactions

For children with Asperger's who have siblings, where in the birth order they fall also plays a role in the family dynamics. Due to genetic factors, a child with AS has an increased probability of having siblings who have developmental, learning, or emotional problems. Certainly, raising an only child with AS is different from having a child with this condition who has one or more sisters or brothers, even if the siblings are neurotypical. The challenges, of course, increase exponentially when one or more siblings have some kind of ASD. The attitude, level of comprehension, and daily behaviors of siblings can be expected to influence both the way children with AS perceive themselves, and their progress. For this reason, clinicians often strongly advocate the involvement of siblings in support groups and individual and family sessions as a regular aspect of the child's treatment plan. Helping a neurotypical brother or sister understand more about a sibling's needs and challenges as well as the appropriate way to help, if he or she is so inclined, can mitigate many potential family problems, like feeling that the sibling with AS gets too much attention or is embarrassing.

Action for Parents

Make a point of helping siblings express their feelings and concerns regarding their brother's or sister's AS.

Financial Concerns

Socioeconomic status and financial attitudes are part of the context in which a child with Asperger's is raised. It must be recognized that, all things being equal, having the financial wherewithal to have assistance at home and afford the best care possible can make a tough situation more manageable. At the same time, however, all the money in the world in and of itself cannot cure AS.

Trying to afford the many services that could assist a child with AS can place severe financial strain on a family—or exceed their resources. Moreover, parental earnings may be foregone as their work hours or careers come in second to meeting their child's needs. This is a disheartening situation with no real answer at this time. Parents in this plight can sometimes find resources through Asperger's advocacy groups, social service and charitable organizations, university training centers, or research grants. Some private practitioners may have sliding scales available for qualified applicants or reserve certain hours for pro bono work. Ideally, parents will not let pride or embarrassment keep them from trying to obtain the help that they and their child need. They should try not to lose sight of this: The worst that can happen is that they'll be turned down and have to keep looking elsewhere. One bright note is that in recent years various courts and legislative authorities throughout the U.S. have increasingly required insurance companies to extend coverage to meet the needs of children with autistic spectrum disorders.[49]

There are times when people who actually do have the means do not get their child the necessary assistance, yet refer to cost as the reason. This may be indicative of a lack of true understanding, empathy, or emotional connection with their child. Also, some parents may have difficulty perceiving the value of nontangible clinical services in the same way they would perceive the value of a material possession such as a luxury car, or an expensive attorney if they were facing a legal problem. For some, especially in the American culture, there is often a mind-set that health services should be free or very low cost. Unfortunately, this expectation is probably not too realistic.

For some, the choice to not seek services that actually are feasible may mask denial, anger, resentment, or anxiety: reactions that a parent may lack insight into or not be ready to address. When parents disagree with each other about allocation of economic resources for their child's evaluation, treatment, and education, one or both can experience high levels of emotional stress, and there is the further risk of a severe marital rift. Sadly, the divorce rate among parents of special needs children is very high,[50] no doubt with financial conflicts as a major contributor to this problem.

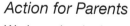

Action for Parents

Work on developing a financial plan that balances needs for services with a realistic appraisal of available resources.

Asperger's Syndrome Outside the Home

Many parents of children with Asperger's syndrome have very understandable concerns about how their children will function, and how others will treat them, when the parents themselves are not present. Still, for children with AS to become as independent as possible, sooner or later they must separate from their parents. They will need to have their own educational and social experiences.

School

In general, school is a challenge for children with Asperger's, even for those who are academically proficient. Their idiosyncratic behaviors and social difficulties make fitting into traditional educational environments problematic for a slew of reasons. They may show indifference to matters of grooming, clothing style, manners, and personal hygiene that can stigmatize them with other students. They frequently do not see any point to the social opportunities the school setting presents.

Unfortunately, children with AS are often vulnerable to actual teasing and bullying from their schoolmates. However, it can be confusing when they report these kinds of problems because they may also be prone to mistakenly believing they are under attack, due to difficulty differentiating truly malicious teasing from normal joking around. One child with AS might consider a relatively mild negative comment from a peer as unforgivable and a reason to stop attending school; another might fail to realize when he or she is in a truly risky situation with another student; still another might be prone to both these errors of social perception.

Especially when they are being taught a new, nonpreferred subject, children with AS benefit from being given a structure with specific steps to follow at first. Many seem to learn more effectively with methods of instruction that involve visual cues and hands-on experiences. They may get quite frustrated and not progress to the best of their ability if they are taught in ways that are too abstract or are predominantly reliant upon auditory processes. Unfortunately for these children, standard methods of teaching rely heavily on auditory-processing abilities. This approach becomes even more the norm as children progress from the lower grades to high school and beyond.

Children with AS often manifest problems in organization, prioritizing, time management, and sequencing that may adversely affect academic performance. Because they are fact oriented rather than "gist" oriented, even very adept students with AS often start having academic issues in the higher grades, especially when it comes to producing written work that requires more facility in understanding and expressing abstract concepts. They often resist doing schoolwork or homework that they do not perceive as having a specific purpose for them; if asked, they might describe these tasks as being pointless wastes of time.

Students with AS are often quite perplexing and/or frustrating to educators, particularly to those who lack enough experience with this population and may tend to misinterpret typical Asperger's behaviors as purposefully disruptive, disrespectful, uninterested, or lacking motivation, or even as reflective of negligent or incompetent parenting. Of course, that is not to say that there are no educators who find the learning challenges of children with AS fascinating; many do.

Working on group projects—that by definition require teamwork, the ability to compromise, and facility in understanding others' points of view—presents a special challenge for children with AS because of their social deficits. When faced with this situation, they may be prone to one of two extremes: not participating at all or trying to monopolize the group. If a child with AS also has a specific learning disability, like a problem in reading comprehension, the already daunting challenges of adjusting to school are further compounded.

Luckily, over the years many schools have become more Asperger's-friendly. Some schools make a point of providing education about AS to their staff. A variety of accommodations to help children with AS adjust to school academically, behaviorally, and emotionally are available in many school districts and are sometimes legally mandated.[51] Examples

53

of possible accommodations that might be necessary include extended test times, separate testing locations, individual or classroom aides, note-takers, in-school counseling, in-class aides (shadows), visual prompts and schedules, and in-school social skills/personal counseling. For children who have graphomotor problems, technological assistance can come in the form of a laptop computer or other word-processing device. One note of caution: Technological accommodations have the potential to backfire if a child becomes too dependent upon them or is overly distracted by their use.

Accommodations may be easier to obtain in public schools because of legal requirements,[52] but many private schools are willing to help as well. Parents and educators, however, need to resist overaccommodating a child and risking excessive dependency, which can actually impede long-term growth and provide an illusory sense of gain. Although parents of children with AS understandably may be concerned about labeling and stigmatizing, being open about diagnosis and providing educators with the most accurate medical and psychological information possible is most often the wisest policy. Some schools may even have an AS teaching specialist who is available to support a child's general education. Other schools will allow parents to bring in outside experts to provide support and training.

If parents experience difficulty obtaining the necessary accommodations for their child, they may want to consider the involvement of a parent advocate (a person who is specially trained to help parents navigate through the educational world) or, if they cannot obtain satisfaction, consulting an attorney with expertise in children with special needs and due process procedures in schools might be an option.

Action for Parents

Periodically review your child's individualized educational plan to ensure that it meets current needs and supports appropriate planning for the future.

Homeschooling

Given the difficulties that many children with Asperger's face in school and the resulting pain that parents feel, it is understandable and very tempting to just want out of the system. Some parents choose homeschooling as an alternative. Reasons vary from frustration with regular schools, to providing a safe haven from teasing and bullying and negative social influences, to the belief that an involved parent can be more effective in meeting a child's unique educational needs.

Before deciding to homeschool, however, parents are well advised to carefully weigh the long- and short-term pros and cons. Given the potential risks, it is also a good idea to have a frank conference about this matter with the child's teacher and educational support team, as well as any clinicians or agencies that have expertise in these matters. Although fortunately there are good social networking opportunities in many areas for homeschoolers, providing adequate and real-life social experiences might be especially difficult for homeschooled children with AS. It also takes a lot of practical know-how, drive, persistence, and frustration tolerance to meet the range of needs of homeschooled children with AS, both academic and social. Parents who are unprepared or not emotionally suited to homeschooling need to be honest with themselves before taking their child out of a more traditional educational setting. Children with AS, even very bright ones, can easily become lost in a fantasy world of video games or TV that further compromises their potential, or even worse, results in significant levels of regression.

Residential Therapeutic Placements and Wilderness Programs

There are cases when the best option might involve placement of a child with Asperger's in a residential therapeutic educational setting or wilderness program (also known as an outdoor behavioral health program, this is not the same as a "boot camp"). That is to say, if local school possibilities have been exhausted, homeschooling is not a viable alternative, or the child is too socially impaired, psychologically compromised, or aggressive/oppositional-defiant, there may be no other choice.

Placing a child with AS in the appropriate residential therapeutic school or wilderness program is a complex matter; some parents choose to use the services of an experienced and knowledgeable educational consultant to explore options and facilitate a good match for the child and the family. Of course, residential schools and wilderness programs (not to mention educational consultants) tend to be quite costly, which impedes the placement of many children in need. In some instances, the cost of this type of placement may be shouldered by the school district or some other public agency. Choosing to place one's child in a residential therapeutic school or wilderness program is likely going to be an emotionally charged issue for parents; it can feel as if they are abandoning their child or have failed as parents. If parents have to make this difficult life decision, however, it is more constructive for them to focus on how willing they are to do whatever it takes to support their child's development and give him or her the best possible chance to thrive.

Translating the progress made in the structure of a residential or wilderness program back to the home environment is especially hard for individuals with AS. Therefore, it is of paramount importance that well-trained staff specifically address this issue during the course of these programs.

Action for Parents

When considering a placement, make sure to consult with knowledgeable sources in order to prevent making an unfortunate choice. Relying on an Internet search or the advice of friends and family is probably not going to result in obtaining the correct information.

Summer Camps and Programs

As the prevalence and needs of children with Asperger's and their parents have been more understood, there are more camps that not only provide a safe, enjoyable summer break but also have specially trained staff to facilitate activities and experiences that have embedded, or "stealth," therapy. This approach intrinsically assists in the development of skills such as working with a team, making friends, assertiveness/ self-advocacy, coping with authority, and overcoming anxiety. There are also programs that may be specifically targeted to a certain need, like sensorimotor development or intensively working on social language.

While some of these are local programs or day camps, many of the most helpful are sleepaway. Many parents are understandably nervous about entrusting the welfare of their vulnerable child to others away from home, and fears that their child might be teased, physically or sexually mistreated, or miss home too much are common. There may also be the thought that no one can understand this particular child but his or her own parents. While, of course, there are never any guarantees, and the love and caring of parents cannot be replaced or duplicated—even for neurotypical children—the best policy is to research the camp or summer program as well as possible and focus on what the child needs in terms of developing independence, not to mention a break from parents. And, while on this subject, it's possible that parents can benefit from a summer break too; sending a child to camp is nothing to feel overly guilty about. Actually, this time might go a long way toward increasing a depleted energy level and refreshing the ability to maintain a healthy perspective.

What is the most helpful approach if a child with AS does not want to go to a summer camp or program although his or her parents have clearly decided that this is the right choice? Proceeding the same way one would with a child who didn't want to go to school or the dentist, or even participate in a beneficial but nonmandatory physical activity, like a sport, is probably the best option. That is, validating the child's feelings, while making it clear that the parents are going to stick to the decision that is right in the long run is both a caring and constructive way to navigate through this difficult situation.

Social Skills Groups

Enrollment in social skills groups is often an important part of a well-designed, comprehensive intervention plan. Children with AS characteristically do not organically develop lasting and meaningful social connections, especially as they get older and their parents can no longer step in to set up playdates for them. These children are also less likely to be interested in or frequently even capable of participating in typical after-school activities such as competitive sports or even neighborhood pickup games. The result is often increasing withdrawal into solitary, sometimes idiosyncratic pursuits. Participation in social skills groups can give children with AS a structured opportunity to play cooperatively with children they might otherwise never have met, and a chance to learn about typical activities for their age group and have some fun, perhaps even make a lasting friendship, along the way.

Although truly reciprocal and insightful social functioning cannot be broken down into elements to "fix," making improvements in specific areas of functioning can often really help; for example, how far to stand from other children when speaking with them, how to ask another child to play, or how to keep a conversation going. Moreover, these groups can bring parents who feel alone into contact with other parents in similar situations; they can share ideas and resources, maybe over a friendly cup of coffee.

Not all social groups are the same. While some social skills groups are quite structured and didactic, others present a free-form environment in which children can work on their interpersonal abilities. Groups may also differ in terms of leadership; the leader might be a clinical professional, a graduate student, an educator, or another parent or volunteer from the community. These differences may translate to variables like cost and the frequency of sessions. As always, finding the best fit for both children and their parents takes some thought. Some parents worry that their child will copy the behaviors of children in the group that are more atypical than their own. This probably does not occur as often as parents might fear, and even if it does happen, it might assist children in developing an important skill—maintaining their own most appropriate behavior regardless of what others around them might do. Bear in mind that sophisticated social skills group leaders often create challenges and activities that children might not like, but are of benefit to them in the long run; for example, setting up a situation where they have to practice coping with losing a game.

Action for Parents

If you have not done so already, consider the benefits of a social skills group. If you choose to follow through on this idea, set a goal to make your own social plans with another parent whose child is also enrolled.

Educating Children about Asperger's Syndrome

There is no single answer to the question of whether, when, and how to tell children that they have Asperger's syndrome. The response depends on a number of factors, including age, general intellectual level, degree of associated emotional issues, and current stressors. It can be very helpful for a child to learn about AS if information is presented in a skillful, well-timed, and compassionate manner.

Parents may find it worthwhile to discuss this matter with their family physician or developmental/mental health professional, who may provide resources, such as age-appropriate books or videos, that can make introducing and discussing AS a smoother process. If necessary, they can point out reasons to postpone or completely table discussion of this matter. There may be children who are just not able to understand their diagnosis or are so defensive that focusing on it before they are ready would be counterproductive. In such cases, centering discussion and interventions on their specific problems and symptoms may prove more helpful than discussing their diagnosis, at least for the time being.

Some parents may be concerned that they will stigmatize their son or daughter by telling the diagnosis. They may also worry that they will discourage their child; that is, children who know they have a potentially disabling condition will experience a self-fulfilling prophecy and act as if they have one. Parents might also be concerned that making their child feel "different" will result in the child's becoming sad or depressed, or having a lower sense of self-worth.

If the decision is to communicate the diagnosis, the idea is to present information about AS in a straightforward, matter-of-fact, and nonjudgmental manner that is appropriate to a child's age and ability to comprehend. Allowing children the opportunity to ask questions and express their feelings about what they have been told is also recommended. It may help to know that many children suspect that there is something different about them, and knowing the diagnosis may actually provide some relief and allow them to better understand the efforts of those trying to assist them. Some children will have a delayed reaction to learning about AS. That is, a child who seems neutral or accepting at first might begin to verbalize or indirectly manifest signs—for example, being more withdrawn or irritable than usual for no obvious reason—of being upset about the AS label even months later.

An individual child's reaction to learning that he or she has AS is difficult to predict. There can be a varied and wide range of responses from total indifference to crying to angry outbursts, among others. Some children may plead with their parents to remove the diagnosis as if it were an irritating article of clothing that they just want off of them immediately. However, many times children's reactions seem to reflect their parents' feelings. That is, if children sense disappointment or negative reactions from their parents, they are likely to react to the diagnosis with less positivity.

In recent years, there has been a trend toward increasing the education of individuals about the conditions they have, even children. I view this trend favorably; in my experience, children with AS who know and understand their diagnosis fare better in the long run.

Treatment for Asperger's Syndrome

Once the diagnosis of Asperger's syndrome has been made and accepted, it's natural for parents to say, "OK, I understand the problem. Now what can be done to help my child?" The following sections will attempt to respond to this all-important question. Not all children with AS would benefit from the interventions that will be presented, just as some interventions would not be acceptable to some parents. Nevertheless, it seems worthwhile for parents to become well informed about the available options.

Sources of Professional Help

Once the diagnosis of Asperger's is made, the next step is to determine the most helpful approaches to treatment. Sometimes this can be quite confusing, as opinions on best practices often vary, even when they come from well-regarded experts. However, overall, children with AS benefit from a comprehensive approach involving knowledgeable professionals including:

- *Pediatricians/Family physicians/Internists/Nurse practitioners.* These medical professionals assess general health status, perform blood work and other laboratory testing, and help rule out health problems that could be misdiagnosed as AS.

- *Developmental and behavioral pediatricians.* These physicians, highly familiar with normative development and the medical needs of

61

children, have additional certified training in assessing, diagnosing, and treating children with neurodevelopmental problems.

- *Pediatric neurologists.* These medical specialists are certified to diagnose and treat children whose neurological status is compromised in some way. Some pediatric neurologists have a subspecialty in ASDs. The services of pediatric neurologists and child psychiatrists often overlap for those in the autism spectrum, and it may be difficult to decide whom to see. Sometimes follow-up with both is recommended (e.g., if seizures co-occur with a significant psychological condition, like depression or anxiety).

- *Child and adolescent psychiatrists.* It requires very intensive training to assess and treat the emotional and behavioral needs of younger people. These medical doctors are entrusted with having the sophisticated knowledge necessary to prescribe psychotropic medications in a safe, effective, and thoughtful manner.

- *Psychologists.* Professionals in this field who are in practice are generally doctoral-level mental and behavioral health specialists who diagnose, treat, and may conduct formal psychological/ psychoeducational evaluations. They may play a variety of roles with regard to autism spectrum conditions, according to their particular areas of training and expertise. Those who have completed specialized training in conducting neuropsychological assessments are called neuropsychologists. School psychologists are responsible for helping to make sure the proper educational placements and accommodations are made; they may also administer psychological testing and perform other school-related duties.

- *Educators.* Special education teachers, classroom teachers, and school administrators generally have a wide range of experience with children and therefore become expert in spotting anomalies in development and progress in educational and social realms. Finding a tutor with a special education background is often a part of the global plan for children with AS.

- *Speech therapists.* Clinicians who work with speech and language development are often key players in a comprehensive plan for children with AS. Speech therapists work on problems involving fluency, prosody (the rhythms of speech), and pragmatics (social, verbal, and nonverbal communication skills), areas of functioning that tend to affect these children.

- *Audiologists/Ophthalmologists/Optometrists.* It is important to assess hearing and vision as part of the diagnostic process. Both of these issues could be contributory to problems in social functioning that resemble autism spectrum conditions.

- *Occupational therapists.* Occupational therapists (OTs) are skilled in addressing many problems associated with AS. They can assist in addressing sensory problems, physical awkwardness, fine motor skills, balance, and activities of daily living.

- *Physical therapists.* Commonly known as PTs, physical therapists can help children with AS who have gross motor problems. Their work can help individuals in this population learn and enjoy sports, exercise, and other physical activities that are important for their overall development.

- *Behaviorists.* Board-certified behavior analysts are specifically educated and trained in systematically applying behavior therapy concepts to a host of behavioral excesses and deficits. Some specialize in reduction of highly disruptive behaviors (e.g., aggression), others in building social skills.

- *Equine therapists.* Facilitated by an expert, interacting with horses provides a therapeutic experience in nature for children with AS. Horses have an inherent ability to reflect children's social demeanor and behaviors. To get horses to comply or respond, children need to modify their affect, expressed emotions, and behavioral tendencies to make them acceptable to the horse. Since many children with AS like animals, equine therapy is a great way to enhance skills that can be generalized to humans. Further, wearing a helmet, coping with changes in a horse's movements, petting a horse, and other experiences that are part of this therapy may have inherently positive effects.

- *Art therapists.* Sometimes a picture really does tell a thousand words; through art, a visual medium, children can express feelings that they cannot communicate using verbal language. It is self-evident why this approach may be particularly useful for children with AS. For example, having them draw faces with different expressions can help them learn more about their own emotions and perhaps enhance their skill in detecting nonverbal cues in the facial expressions of others.

- *Movement therapists.* Movement therapists can help children with AS improve their ability to connect with their bodies. Body movement, in the form of dancing or playing games that require them to change their postures or gestures, offers a way for children to communicate and express themselves emotionally.

- *Educational counselors/Placement specialists.* When parents cannot locate or determine the living and/or educational resources that their child needs, educational counselors are the people to see. Finding the right educational counselor—one who is experienced with the special requirements for children with AS—is essential. A poorly thought-out or inappropriate placement can be highly detrimental to a child with AS.

Medications

There is no exact psychopharmacological approach for Asperger's, although on a case-by-case basis those with AS may benefit from medications targeting symptoms that cause distress or interfere with their day-to-day lives. Further, medications may help some with AS be more able to participate in other kinds of therapy; for example, by reducing reactivity or anxiety or by increasing their ability to focus.

Medications identified for treatment of individuals with AS have been largely studied in adults, not children, which warrants some caution for prescriptions in this population. Choosing the most appropriate course of action when it comes to medication requires expertise and continued, timely monitoring by qualified and experienced medical professionals; it is easy to underestimate the expertise that goes into saying "I think we should try this kind of medicine." Here are some of the options that could be considered:[53]

- *Selective serotonin reuptake inhibitors (SSRIs).* May help reduce ritualistic behaviors and improve mood, as well as help children with AS adapt more flexibly to new situations. Downside: may increase hyperactivity and potential for other side effects (e.g., headaches). Since there is an ongoing controversy as to whether these agents can trigger suicidal behaviors in certain children, there must be close medical supervision, particularly in the first phase of use.

- *Tricyclic antidepressants.* Used in similar ways as SSRIs; also affect serotonin as well as norepinephrine receptors. Have resulted in the reduction of self-injurious behaviors. Downside: may worsen underlying seizure disorder.

- *Neuroleptics.* Used to reduce stereotyped behaviors and social withdrawal. Also used to control aggressive behaviors, sleep problems, anxiety, and other serious symptoms that are unresponsive to behavioral treatment. Sometimes used to augment the effects of SSRIs. Downside: many potential side effects, such as sedation, cognitive/personality flattening, as well as increased risk for diabetes and disordered movements (the possibility of tardive dyskinesia, a serious, incurable movement condition which, while quite infrequent, must nonetheless be a concern).

- *Atypical neuroleptics.* Newer compounds that target similar symptoms and problems as neuroleptics. Hoped to have fewer side effects than the earlier neuroleptics but in many instances, unfortunately, may have similar downsides.

- *Mood stabilizers.* Typically used to address mood lability (instability) and agitation. There is limited information on the role of mood stabilizers for individuals with AS unless there is a family history of bipolar disorder. Downside: possible weight gain, mental sluggishness.

- *Anxiolytics.* Used to reduce anxiety as well as to lessen activity level, improve sleep, and reduce stereotyped behaviors. Downside: may be addictive when used long-term or be associated with dampening of motivation. Some concerns have been raised that the presence of anxiolytics could potentially interfere with some of the mechanisms (e.g., habituation) by which exposure-based therapies seem to work.

- *Beta-blockers.* Mixed results on the effectiveness of beta-blockers on AS symptoms like excessive anger and tension. Lately, they have been used for ADHD as well. Downside: may cause dizziness.

- *Stimulants.* In AS, these agents may be used to target co-occurring problems in attention and concentration that may resemble ADHD. Although concerns have been raised that psychostimulant medication may create or trigger tics, increase stereotyped behaviors and agitation, adversely affect sleep and appetite, and elicit or exacerbate obsessive-compulsive behaviors, some experts hold that for numerous children with AS, the beneficial effects of this class of medications may frequently outweigh the risks.

For parents, there are a number of important issues to consider when making decisions about the use of psychotropic medications for children with AS. When it comes to this subject, there are likely to be strong emotions for parents, and in many cases for the children themselves. Parents may have misgivings about the use of psychopharmacological interventions, especially with younger children. Worries about immediate side effects and long-term effects are normal. However, parents must also consider the side effects, so to speak, of choosing not to medicate their child; for example, lack of relief for depression or anxiety, disruptive behaviors, level of family conflict, inability to pay attention that prevents the child from progressing socially or academically, and inability to participate in or benefit from other kinds of therapies. The following points can help parents make their own risk-benefit analysis:[54]

- Individuals with AS may be more susceptible to side effects of medications and are less likely to tolerate these side effects. Therefore, prescribers may be limited to using lower dosages than have been found effective for other populations.

- Individuals with AS are less likely to effectively communicate the degree of their discomfort or distress related to a medication's side effects to their treatment provider.

- Medication may not be an appropriate treatment option for all patients with AS. Behavioral and educational interventions are often first-line treatments for children. When used concurrently with pharmacological treatment, psychological and educational approaches might, in certain cases, allow for using the lowest doses possible or for briefer medication trials.

Action for Parents
When it comes to medications, never be afraid to express your concerns. Well-trained professionals will welcome the opportunity to address your questions. If there are issues on your mind about this subject, set up a time when they can be openly discussed with the prescribing clinician(s).

Psychological Approaches

Psychotherapy for children with Asperger's is still evolving. Can talk therapy help children with AS? It depends; if the purpose of the talk is to get them to achieve insight that will lead them to making changes in their lives, experts in the field would likely answer with a resounding no.

It is generally accepted that psychotherapy for children with AS needs to be structured and goal directed to be effective. A major focus for helping children with AS is on improving pragmatics, which means their ability to understand and respond effectively to social contexts.[55] Stress management, problematic emotions and behaviors, and reducing physiological sensitivities are also commonly addressed, as are co-occurring problems like anxiety or depression. Therapists will often involve parents in their child's treatment plan to help them gain a good understanding of the techniques that are being used and learn how to support their child's goals, especially between sessions. Sometimes they may be asked to come in without their son or daughter so that they have a chance to freely express their concerns or work on specific parenting skills.

Psychotherapy is also aimed at increasing behavioral and emotional flexibility—and, hopefully, empathy—so that these children can increase their capacity to interact with others in a more natural manner. Another goal is to establish a "model" relationship with the therapist that can potentially serve as a template for ones in their regular lives, whether present or future. Helping a child with AS learn to create and work toward constructive life goals is also a common aspect of the work in therapy.

Specific exercises are often a key aspect of psychotherapy sessions for those with AS. For instance, to work on decreasing mind-blindness, children with AS might be asked to play a form of Twenty Questions to practice decoding another person's statements and behavior. Similarly, they might be engaged in a role-reversal exercise that involves pretending they are the therapist and the therapist is a person with AS that they are trying to help better understand social situations.

A clinical challenge is to try to influence those with AS toward positive social adaptations without appearing too critical or judgmental; for example, a high-functioning teenager with AS wore a huge fanny pack that made him stick out like a sore thumb in school. When his therapist first suggested that he stop wearing the fanny pack, the boy became angry, accusing the therapist of "not accepting me as I am." Over the next few sessions this individual was asked to challenge this self-defeating

68

perspective and collect data about how he was perceived with and without his fanny pack on.

Because insufficient motivation and awareness (insight) is an issue for so many children with AS, psychological and behavioral therapeutic approaches must take this into consideration at the outset of any course of treatment. Fortunately, there are many strategies that can be used to address these problems. Some children with AS are more able to see the connection between going for therapy and learning how to lead a happier, more typical life; others are less able to do so. For these latter children, using tangible rewards to increase their willingness to cooperate with their treatment plan may prove helpful. Although it doesn't seem too "therapeutic," for moderately resistant children, motivation may need to be further established by withholding preferred items or activities until they become adequately compliant. Unfortunately, some children with AS are so opposed to psychotherapy that forcing the situation is counterproductive, and other options may need to be considered to get them the help they need.

Action for Parents

Make sure to ask any questions you may have regarding your child's psychological treatment, just as you would for a medical approach.

Prognosis for Asperger's Syndrome

A prognosis is a prediction regarding the expected course of an illness or other kind of health problem. The question of whether a child with Asperger's syndrome will grow up to have a normal life is one of the most difficult for any clinician to answer. Parents ask this question in many different ways, sometimes bluntly, and sometimes so disguised that it is up to the clinician to decode what they really want to know. It is a question that taps into the deepest kinds of parental emotions—for example, anxiety and anger; it is also a question that can elicit feelings in the therapist, who has to respond in a meaningful, caring manner that both reflects the child's current presentation and offers appropriate hope and guidance. It is not an easy task for therapists to strike the balance between maintaining both the necessary clinical distance to be professional and the humanity to comfort a distressed parent.

Just as with many health conditions, making a prognosis about AS has elements of both science and art. Consequently, a perfectly reliable and valid prognosis is impossible for any practitioner, no matter how qualified or experienced, to offer. Any clinician experienced with AS can tell of dire prognoses that did not turn out to be correct, as well as better prognoses that turned out to be overly optimistic. Keeping this in mind, here is a summary of what is known about the prognosis for AS at present.[56]

- More intensive behavioral interventions implemented when the child is very young seem to result in better outcomes than interventions introduced when the child is older. Put simply, the earlier the intervention, the better the prognosis, so earlier detection is needed; at present, the average age of diagnosis is eleven,[57] which highlights the need for earlier "case finding" and improved early screening and assessment methods.

- Psychotherapy for individuals with AS appears most effective when it is structured and focused on developing social and emotional skills as well as practical strategies for coping with daily life. Interventions that target social competence (such as social skills training) are most effective when they are generalized to the child's everyday situations and environments.

- Psychological and behavioral treatment tends to be more successful for those who have good verbal skills that enable them to more actively participate in their own treatment.

- Intelligence also appears to moderate intervention effects for individuals with autism spectrum conditions; children with lower IQs tend to respond less well to interventions than children with higher IQs.

- Family involvement plays an important role in the success of treatment. Parents of children with autism spectrum conditions are often at increased risk for the psychological and physical effects of chronic stress due to their role as caregivers. Without proper support for the parents, treatment effects may be minimized for their children.

Treatment failure may also result from not properly implementing a comprehensive treatment approach. In 2008, Karen Toth and Bryan H. King wrote: "The National Research Council and the Committee on Educational Interventions for Children with Autism have identified critical variables for treatment planning, including prioritizing goals based on core challenges in social communication, establishing proactive approaches to problem behaviors, individualizing modes of instruction, implementing supports across contexts, planning for transitions, addressing psychiatric comorbidity, and providing family support and education."[58]

How do those who are diagnosed with AS appear if they have made significant improvements? Well, less "Aspergery." They may have a sort of dual awareness; at once realizing their differentness but at the same time also being able to engage in the behaviors that allow them to function more effectively and fit in better with the neurotypical world. They often take pains to make sure their comments and attire are not too discrepant from those they interact with. In addition, they seem to have a good sense of humor when they realize they have been too literal or self-absorbed. They may not feel any need to hide their diagnosis; they can be very proud of their achievement and wish to help others who are not so fortunate. Finally, parents can take heart that many children who received timely, consistent, and effective interventions and appropriate supports have progressed well beyond expectations.

Can some children who received a diagnosis of AS at one point no longer be diagnosed with this condition later on? It does happen, perhaps more so among those who had fewer or less severe co-occurring conditions. The question remains whether it is due to a faulty initial diagnosis, changes in diagnostic criteria, or actual improvements.[59]

When Children with Asperger's Syndrome Become Adults

Lately, more attention is being paid to what happens to children with Asperger's syndrome as they grow up. Adults with even the milder forms of AS who have received insufficient intervention are at risk for inadequate or problematic social lives, even if they have been able to attain some sort of relationship or viable career. Actually, it is often not AS itself but heightened levels of anxiety, depression, behavioral problems, or conflicts in relationships that leads to the initial consultation for high achievers with this condition.

The following information is noted about teens and adults with AS:[60]

- For a child, becoming a teen may lead to better functioning in communication and social interactions. However, ritualistic/stereotyped behaviors may not change significantly due to maturation alone. Adolescents may find puberty confusing and will often need guidance in addressing topics such as body changes, dating, sexuality, and gender identity.

- Seizure disorder, most commonly complex-partial epilepsy, may develop as a child becomes a teen or an adult. However, the incidence is quite low, especially when intelligence is in the average range, and it is quite common that the seizures are temporary, rather than chronic.

- There seems to be no significant difference in mortality rates between adults with and without AS.

- There may be a certain pattern of psychiatric disorders that develop in individuals with AS, including risks for depression and deterioration of the thought process.

- There is scant data to support the general notion that a person with AS is more likely to commit crimes. Although there are a number of case studies that describe crimes committed by people with AS, these crimes tend to be largely related to their specialized interests, rigidity, or limited understanding of social interactions. In some cases, the crimes were actually instigated by another individual. As there is no epidemiological data available, no general statement can be made about the prevalence of criminal behaviors among people with AS. Nevertheless, parents need to be aware that in many instances, having a diagnosis, even a very well-substantiated one, of AS is unlikely to be considered an excuse, or even much of a mitigating factor, if a crime is committed. And if a person with AS is found guilty of a crime and incarcerated, adjusting to prison life is exponentially more difficult, just as one might expect.

When it comes to behaviors that can result in arrest, injury to self or others, or long-term health problems, the presence of minimal (or complete absence of) physical stigmata can actually be a problem. The ability to present a facade of fitting in, no matter how marginally, can be associated with children getting into situations that are over their heads and interacting with others who do not have their best interests in mind. AS doesn't make a child immune from social issues like crime, gambling, licit or illicit drug use, and promiscuity or health concerns like obesity or cigarettes. For those with AS, excessively consuming drugs or alcohol is probably going to compromise their social awareness, judgment, and perhaps motivation even further. Even if by drinking or getting high, they are trying to act like peers they think are "cool," this attempt will likely backfire and just make them more vulnerable to being exploited or, at the very least, the butt of jokes or pranks. Furthermore, substance abuse inherently increases the risk of triggering or worsening seizures, anxiety, depression, and disturbances of thinking and perception. Also, if they are taking medications, there is the chance of untoward interactions effects as well as loss of clinical efficacy.

A major emerging area of concern is the potential vulnerability of those with AS to become enmeshed in illegal activities on the Internet (e.g., underage pornography).[61] This possibility creates a particular dilemma because so many children with AS are attracted to computers, and especially the Internet. Segregating a child with AS from the computer or Internet entirely to eliminate even remotely potential problems is no real solution and is unnecessary unless a specific risk has been determined to exist.

Takeaway Action

Think about the three most important points you learned from this section. Decide on the first way to use what you have learned thus far, whether it is a positive change in perspective or beginning to implement a specific goal.

Section II
Obsessive-Compulsive Behaviors

As knowledge about Asperger's syndrome has grown, the importance of learning more about obsessive-compulsive behaviors (OCBs) is becoming more apparent to parents, just as it has for practitioners. Most children with AS will manifest OCBs in one way or another, at one time or another, or at one level of severity or another, and the failure to understand and address these behaviors can create a bottleneck, drastically stifling the child's potential development.

Parents may feel ambivalent toward reading about this topic. Having mixed feelings is totally natural, but it is important be to aware of them. When we don't recognize the negative side of any desire to learn or change, it is easier for those detrimental factors to affect our behavior. For example, if we want to change our eating habits, it's important to recognize, rather than deny, how tasty unhealthful treats can be. Acknowledging that we are actively deciding to sacrifice immediate gratification in the interest of achieving our goals only adds to strengthening our resolve.

Providing an exact definition for OCBs is a problem. That's because there is some inherent overlap with other clinical terms such as fixation, perseveration, or stereotyped behavior (this is discussed more in a later section). However, most of the bases seem to be covered by these three points: (1) the behavior is characterized by repetitiveness and lack of actual necessity, aside from immediate gratification or relief from discomfort; (2) there is an internal push toward continuing this behavior despite negative consequences; and (3) attempts to change this behavior meet with resistance and/or distress. In a child with AS, determining whether there is a corresponding obsession is often not possible. For experienced practitioners and very knowledgeable parents, it's often a case of "I know it when I see it."

To help you focus your attention further and continue to develop a good foundation of knowledge, decide whether each of the following statements is true or false:

- Children choose to engage in OCBs.

- Children will always grow out of engaging in their OCBs; it's just a phase they are going through.

- Bad parenting is the cause of OCBs.

- OCBs are impossible to change.

- There is no choice; parents must go along with all of their child's OCBs.

The fact is, all of these statements are false.

Action for Parents

Clarifying our reasons for seeking information and help is an important step in any process that involves learning. Realizing why we are in search of more knowledge can support our motivation to make, and keep on making, positive changes even when we encounter frustrating obstacles. This is as good a time as any to specifically consider your own motivations.

Obsessive-Compulsive Disorder

Obsessive-compulsive disorder (OCD), in its classic form, is a complex, heterogeneous neurobiological condition that overlaps with many other clinical entities and affects many millions of people worldwide. In the DSM, OCD is presently classified under anxiety disorders; some researchers and practitioners, however, wonder if OCD is distinctive enough to merit its own category. It is a serious condition not to be confused with regular worries or habits that people joke about, as in "I was really OCD today."

This disorder is typified by intrusive thoughts or worries, images, and sensations and/or repetitive, ritualistic mental or overt behaviors that reduce discomfort or anxiety.[62] As with Asperger's syndrome, there are many notables who have either publicly stated that they have OCD or are suspected of having OCD on the basis of historical data: soccer star David Beckham, TV personalities Howie Mandel and Marc Summers, billionaire aviator Howard Hughes, and composer Ludwig van Beethoven, to name just a few. OCD has also become a popular subject in movies and on TV. Interestingly, even people without OCD may feel comforted by performing certain everyday behaviors in the same way, which can give us all at least a modicum of insight into this condition.

One way to keep the difference between obsessions and compulsions straight is that obsessions tend to increase anxiety or discomfort while compulsions tend to decrease anxiety or discomfort, at least in the short run. There may be some cases of "pure" obsessions, like a melody that repetitively and intrusively comes into someone's mind but, in general, obsessions result in some kind of relief-seeking mental activity or other kind of avoidance behavior. There is a significant third major element in OCD: doubting. Doubting is akin to not believing one's own eyes and ears.[63] It is related to the indecisiveness, slowness, and checking behaviors frequently observed along with OCD.

Statistics regarding OCD are somewhat more clear-cut and accepted than those pertaining to AS. The lifetime prevalence rate of OCD is somewhere around 2.5%, with somewhat higher rates for females.[64] Recent estimates are that about one in two hundred children have OCD.[65] It seems to have a dual peak age of onset, at around age ten and then in the early twenties;[66] however, earlier onset is more common for males. Children as young as two or three years of age may be diagnosable with OCD,[67] and many, many adults recall having manifested their first OCD symptoms during their early life. There is no known cure for this disorder, but recent advances in cognitive-behavioral and psychopharmacological treatments have greatly helped improve the prognosis and quality of life of many sufferers. More than half of the children and adolescents who receive evidence-based OCD treatment seem to have a good chance of achieving meaningful levels of improvement.[68] While becoming totally symptom-free in the long term is still an uncommon result, those with good insight into their symptoms appear to do best.[69] Particularly worth noting for parents: Positive family involvement has been determined to be an important element in improving outcomes.[70]

Common symptoms involve obsessions about cleanliness, harm, symmetry, and whether one has done something morally wrong, even in a seemingly very minor way. Frequently occurring compulsions include excessive washing, cleaning, checking, arranging, and list making. Compulsions can take the form of rituals and crystallize into habits, or avoidance behaviors, over time. Eating disorders, which include anorexia nervosa, bulimia, and binge eating disorder, appear to have some commonalities with OCD but also key differentiating aspects. It seems worth noting that the presence of early obsessive-compulsive symptoms may be a notable risk factor for developing a specific eating disorder during adolescence.[71]

Compulsions may or may not relate logically to obsessions; thus, a child with fears about dirt might be an excessive hand washer, which makes some sense, but might also have a fear-neutralizing mental ritual that involves repeating the words "Dirt is safe," which is nonsensical.

Most often, individuals with OCD are able to recognize that their worries are irrational; however, this is not necessarily true of all people who have OCD. Those who lack an adequate level of insight about their OCD are said to exhibit higher "overvalued ideation." Young children may lack a set of norms that provide a means of comparison for recognizing whether concerns are reasonable.[72] Also, when OCD is very, very severe, or has been present for a long time without appropriate intervention, rationality about one's symptoms can deteriorate.

Although pediatric OCD resembles the adult form in many respects, children are more likely to describe their issues as worries, show more waxing and waning of symptoms, and have more of a tendency to display certain behaviors; for example, having to touch another person in a specific way or engage in ritualistic behaviors before going to bed, like having to hear "I love you" from their parents a certain number of times. Although there are many routines and rituals that are normal during certain stages of childhood, when they are observed along with a high level of hypersensitivity to touch and taste, a predisposition to developing OCD might be present.[73] Additionally, another possible early warning sign of OCD appears to be present when a child whose routines or rituals are interrupted or prevented demonstrates excessive reactivity.

There are a number of conditions that, over the years, have often been thought to be in the spectrum of OCD.[74] They include:

• *Body dysmorphic disorder.* This disorder involves obsession with a trivial or actually nonexistent flaw in one's physical appearance; the most common issues are with the nose, skin, and hair. Those affected often display an extremely strong belief that their appearance concerns are accurate. Rather than consulting mental health practitioners, they are prone to seeking out surgical or dermatological treatments that frequently provide only temporary relief.

• *Hypochondriasis (health anxiety).* This condition involves obsession about having a serious illness that is not actually present or is unconfirmed even after repeated medical examinations. Those affected misinterpret benign physiological sensations or changes—like new freckles—as certain signs that they are very sick. They are prone to compulsively examining their bodies for problems, or taking their temperature or blood pressure, or "doctor-shopping" for reassurance.

• *Obsessive-compulsive personality disorder.* This condition is characterized by perfectionism, rigidity, need for control, and excessive expectations that others live up to their unrelentingly and unrealistically high standards. People with this disorder often do not perceive that their own attitudes and behaviors are the reason for

79

any interpersonal conflicts or failures they experience; they tend to attribute such difficulties to the shortcomings of others.

- *Hoarding.* Acquiring excessive amounts of tangible items or "information" and/or having an inability to discard them constitute the essence of this problem. Some hoarders accumulate items that seem valueless, like used cans; others fixate on items, like knick-knacks or paintings, that might seem reasonable except that they are collected in unreasonable quantities and displayed very poorly. In the past, hoarding was often thought to be in the realm of OCD-related conditions. Recently, this perspective was challenged to the extent that hoarding might now be considered as a condition in its own right in new versions of the DSM.

Distinguishing Obsessive-Compulsive Behaviors from Obsessive-Compulsive Disorder

Social issues are common in OCD but less severe than in Asperger's. However, even experts might sometimes have difficulty distinguishing obsessive-compulsive behaviors occurring in the context of AS from problems in social functioning that are secondary to classic OCD. Both OCD and OCBs might include doubting, the need for control, behavioral rigidities, the need for sameness, perfectionism, slowed functioning, and avoidance behaviors. However, in comparison with what is typical in OCD, OCBs may be less likely to be connected to a specific catastrophic cognition and are also less likely to have an extensive cognitive structure, meaning that very complicated and analytic thinking about the various aspects of the problem will not be as prevalent. Although presenting similarly at first examination, an OCB tends not to progress in the snowballing manner often characteristic of OCD. Similarly, the avoidance behaviors in OCBs frequently are less complicated, more specific, and less likely to generalize than in OCD.

For example, a young girl with OCD may have a ritual about touching corners of furniture as she passes by. She fears that if she doesn't do this she may get ill or magically cause harm to someone she loves. A person with AS, in contrast, may engage in the same outward behavior but not experience the same kind of fearful thoughts or worsening generalization and anxiety over time. If a child with AS has an obsession or compulsion concerning a blue hat, it is more likely to stay specific to the blue hat than to become attached to hats in general or the color blue, as might occur in OCD. As might be expected, compared to those with typical OCD, children with AS show a greater tendency to have obsessive preoccupations with specific subjects or items.

Even for experienced clinicians, it may be hard to exactly distinguish between an OCB and a stereotyped or rigid, "rule-bound" behavior, fixation, or obsessive-compulsive personality style (having an orderly, controlling manner can develop in those with OCD as a compensatory coping style). When older, higher-functioning individuals with AS may actually display many overlapping features with those who have various personality disorders. The perfectionism, rigidity, idiosyncrasies, and lack of social engagement associated with AS may also be found among those with obsessive-compulsive, avoidant, or schizoid types of personality disorders. The difference is that these people do not have the intense restricted interests, literality, mind-blindness, or other truly defining characteristics of AS.

Level of distress is often another differentiating factor. Those with OCD generally abhor their symptoms and feel as if their condition is not really part of them. It's almost as if an alien entity or bully has taken unwanted control of their thoughts and behavior. As might be expected given the nature of AS, this discrepancy between experience and self-concept is less characteristic of individuals with OCBs. In a way, for those with AS, OCBs are usually part of them, and maybe even a part regarded as special or desirable. This perception creates a major problem for treatment. When distress or insight are lacking, one is far less likely to seek or be accepting of help. Typically, OCBs cause much more distress for others than for the children who have them. This said, let's remember that it is entirely possible that someone with AS would also meet diagnostic criteria for OCD in its classic form.

Causes of Obsessive-Compulsive Behaviors

The exact cause of obsessive-compulsive behaviors in a particular instance is unknown, just as is the case with Asperger's syndrome. Nevertheless, theories abound. In general, it is thought that there is an underlying genetic and biological basis, although factors such as family environment, stress, and certain types of head injuries or illnesses may also play a role. It may turn out that there are numerous factors that interact in complex ways to result in this problem.

It is seeming more possible that childhood infections could be related to the onset of OCD-like symptoms in some cases. There is a condition called PANDAS (pediatric autoimmune neuropsychiatric disorder associated with streptococci) that, while somewhat controversial, may be important to rule out when a child abruptly develops obsessions/compulsions, tics, poor attention, impulse-control problems, and poorer handwriting. Determining the presence of this condition requires a blood test, although there is not a clear consensus regarding the implications for treatment if results are positive. An alternative concept is that a strep infection, like any other stressor, might trigger an outbreak of obsessive-compulsive disorder in a child who is inherently vulnerable to an onset of this condition, or who already has it and just has not been accurately diagnosed yet.[75] Just recently, the concept of PANDAS is being reconceptualized—not without controversy similar to that surrounding the possible changes to the diagnosis of AS discussed in an earlier section—to that of PANS (pediatric acute neuropsychiatric syndrome), or even CANS (childhood acute-onset neuropsychiatric syndrome).[76]

While it is understandable that many parents experience a deep need to find out the exact cause of their child's OCBs, this need may result in a wild goose chase for the so-called magic bullet. This search may waste valuable time and resources, and potentially lead to interventions that are at best unsubstantiated and at worst exploitative or harmful. When it comes to OCBs, focusing on the "how-to" about making progress is generally much more rewarding then getting mired in the quagmire of the "how come?"

Examples of Obsessive-Compulsive Behaviors

A complete list of all the possible obsessive-compulsive symptoms would be extremely long (possibly never-ending), but some of the more typical examples prevalent among those with Asperger's syndrome include the following:[77]

- Repetitive questions
- Excessive reassurance seeking
- Avoiding saying yes or no
- Watching the same videos or playing the same games
- Sitting in the same seat
- Washing and cleaning rituals
- Lining up, placing, or ordering various items
- Being first in line
- Forbidding others to move or touch one's possessions
- Opening and closing doors
- Needing symmetry
- Having to measure the size of various items (e.g., cups, rooms)
- Turning lights on and off
- Perfectionistic writing
- Wearing the same clothing or accessories over and over
- Repeating movie, electronic gaming, or TV dialogue
- Insisting on sleeping with the same toys or stuffed animals; having to have pillows or blankets exactly placed
- Having to hear or avoid certain words or sounds
- Insisting on traveling certain routes

- Hoarding old or useless items (e.g., business cards, gum wrappers)

- Restricted interests (talking and/or reading about certain selected, narrow subjects, such as politics, obituaries, sports, superheroes, or astronomy)

- Rituals concerning foods and eating (excessive concern with texture, colors, warmth, brand, types of cups, plates, or silverware)

Action for Parents
Identify any possible OCBs that you have observed in your child.

Is It "Bad" Behavior or Obsessive-Compulsive Behavior?

When a child takes an undesirable action, parents often wonder whether it is a behavior (meaning purposeful misconduct) or part of the disorder. An example would be children who refuse to stop listening to the same annoying song over and over again, no matter how many times they have been told to stop. In most cases, trying to categorize the action is less useful than (1) holding the children appropriately accountable for listening to their parents' directives despite what their obsessive-compulsive behaviors "tell" them; and (2) considering the functionality of the behavior.

As the word itself implies, functionality refers to an examination of the value and meaning of a particular behavior; whether that behavior results in a reward (e.g., attention, relief) or not (e.g., being ignored, distress). Analyzing the functionality of OCBs is an important part of developing effective treatment plans. Not every one of a child's OCBs has to have the same functionality; for example, checking if a door is open to the correct degree may reduce discomfort, while repetitive "video talk" may provide physiological gratification.

Obsessive-compulsive behaviors may serve some of these functions:

- Controlling the environment (getting parents to sit in certain places in the living room)

- Decreasing interaction with new stimuli (avoidance behaviors when introduced to new people)

- Reducing discomfort (washing repeatedly until feeling "totally clean")

- Providing gratification (getting a good feeling from twirling items in a specific pattern; this may be linked to the release of pleasure-causing neurotransmitters, or brain chemicals, like endorphins)

Understanding more about the functionality of OCBs as they occur in an individual child with Asperger's syndrome can be incorporated into their treatment plan; managing certain contingencies, meaning rewards and consequences, can be very helpful. For example, a child can earn a reward for tolerating discomforts for longer periods of time.

Whatever the initial functionality of the child's OCBs might be, or the myriad factors leading to their acquisition, over time the avoidance of discomfort tends to be what maintains the presence and generalization of these behaviors. In a sense, this is what takes place over the progression of addictive disorders, like alcoholism. Initially, drinking might serve a variety of purposes, like creating a pleasant buzz or reducing social anxiety. However, if the consumption of alcohol becomes habitual, avoiding aversive withdrawal symptoms is usually the contingency that matters most. This is another way to comprehend why learning how to tolerate exposure to discomfort and refrain from avoidance behaviors is so essential in the treatment of OCBs.

Action for Parents

Consider how interpreting annoyingly repetitive verbalizations or actions as "bad" behaviors rather than OCBs may have affected the course of your parenting decisions.

How Do Children Describe What Having Obsessive-Compulsive Behaviors Is Like?

Of course, many children are too young or lack the self-awareness or expressive language to explain what obsessive-compulsive behaviors feel like to them. But when children are able to verbalize what having OCBs feels like, many explain:

- "It's like having a crazy person in your head."
- "It's like having a bad case of the worries."
- "It's like feeling you have to do something you don't really want to do."
- "It's like having to do something that no one else understands."

However, children might also respond:

- "It's just the way I am; I can't describe it."
- "I don't know what you're talking about."

Some children will never respond to this kind of question, for reasons ranging from "won't" to "can't." It's often hard to know what the true reason is for the lack of explanation. There are cases when children have to get a "just right" feeling or sensation that is extremely difficult for them to communicate about or for others to really comprehend.

Common Issues Associated with Obsessive-Compulsive Behaviors

A triad of obsessive-compulsive behaviors, ADHD, and tics is a commonly occurring clinical phenomenon. Similarly, in Asperger's syndrome, OCBs characteristically intermingle with other problems to various degrees, sometimes mildly, but at worst being like an earthquake that triggers a tsunami, leading to flooding that results in widespread destruction of property and lives. As with any negative and potentially spiraling process, recognizing the key elements as soon as possible can lead to strategies that can arrest its progression. This next section pertains to some of the problems that can add to the complexity of addressing OCBs successfully.

Oppositional Behaviors and Aggression

It's already been noted how oppositional behaviors might be misinterpreted as "bad" behaviors. However, this does not mean that actual oppositional-defiance and aggressiveness cannot be associated with obsessive-compulsive behaviors for some children.[78] In particular, children whose rituals are prevented may become so anxious or frustrated that they hit, kick, or become negativistic or explosive in other ways. The difficulties in social understanding that typify AS compound this problem greatly. Oppositional-defiance and aggressiveness become even greater issues during later childhood and the transition to adolescence, when size and strength increases.

This area illustrates how OCBs can be highly detrimental to family relationships; it is very difficult for parents, siblings, or other relatives to have to cope with behaviors that can quickly escalate into verbal and/or physical confrontations. It is no wonder that some parents, knowing the risks of how a child who doesn't get his or her way might behave, make the choice to enable OCBs.

Action for Parents

Is there any possibility that you may be confusing oppositional behaviors with OCBs? If so, consider how bearing this in mind as you respond to problem behaviors might be beneficial.

Anxiety and Depression

It's been noted earlier how anxiety and depression are often associated with Asperger's. Unfortunately, the same negative emotions are also familiar co-occurring problems with OCBs.[79] At its core, anxiety concerns fears and worries but also relates to body tension and nervous cognitions (e.g., "what if" thinking), and difficulty coping with uncertainty and ambiguity. Signs of depression include persistent feelings of sadness (sometimes stated as "boredom" by children), negative changes in eating or sleeping pattern, loss of interest in preferred activities, self-critical thinking, social withdrawal, hopelessness and helplessness, and poor self-image. When children are depressed, helping them fight OCBs becomes even more challenging. Depression is often associated with perfectionism, the subject of the next section.

A side note: Problems giving definitive responses, like yes and no, may be misinterpreted as a sign of lack of confidence, even a depressed mood, for children with AS. Actually, for these children saying things like "maybe" or "I'm not sure" is often more of an indication of doubting, which is a core feature of obsessive-compulsive conditions.

Perfectionism

Perfectionism is also commonly associated with OCBs. At times, it is the pursuit of excellence carried to a self-defeating extreme; at times, it appears to be more like an automatic push toward exactitude with no real long-term purpose. For example, some children excessively erase or rip up their schoolwork if they perceive they have made even a trivial mistake. Others will spend inordinate amounts of time trying to figure out a homework example. Still others will not deviate from the literal "truth" one iota. Some of these children can become extremely self-critical if they feel they have not lived up to their own or an authority figure's standards. Moreover, children with AS often lack awareness as to what appropriate standards of excellence should be. Striving for excellence, in distinction to perfection, is associated with having a wider set of interests and goals that appear to have real-life value (e.g., performing at a high level in a sport or on an instrument versus memorizing the birth dates of all the U.S. presidents) as well as a sense of joy, rather than anxiety or constricted emotional expression, following an achievement.

Tics, Tourette's Syndrome, and Repetitive Body-Focused Behaviors

The term *Tourettic OCD* refers, as the name implies, to a clinical entity characterized by an interrelated combination of tics and obsessive-compulsive symptoms.[80] In the Asperger's population, it is not unusual to see tics, which are semivoluntary, repetitive, intrusive motor or vocal/verbal behaviors,[81] often occurring alongside OCBs. The worst thing parents can do is to try to get their children to stop their tics by constantly pointing them out, or by punishing or making a child feel ashamed. Sometimes a child will tic more freely in front of one parent than the other. This does not mean that the parent seeing fewer tics is doing something right; in fact, it may be just the opposite. Even children with severe tics may be able to suppress them temporarily in the presence of someone whose reaction they are anxious about or fear, but afterward when they feel more comfortable or accepted, they may have a tic "attack."

Examples of common tics include excessive eye blinking, shrugging, mouth widening, grabbing one's crotch, sniffing, and throat clearing. When both vocal/verbal and motor tics are present and have lasted more than one year, Tourette's syndrome (TS) is diagnosed. One of the most difficult aspects of TS to contend with is coprolalia, which refers to compulsive, often explosive cursing.[82] Fortunately, only a relatively small percentage of those with TS ever experience this problem. Also, a substantial number of those with tics or TS will experience a lasting and marked lessening of their symptoms by early adulthood.[83] While there is no perfect treatment for tics or TS, certain medications can provide relief, as can a comprehensive intervention approach including habit reversal training, exposure therapy, and relaxation exercises,[84] as well as other psychological interventions, including parent guidance.

Even when it might be the best policy, ignoring tics, especially when they are highly inappropriate socially, is frequently very difficult for parents. Nonetheless, this is generally the best option, as parental comments and other reactions, no matter how well intended, can potentially increase stress, which in turn tends to result in more tics.

The precise boundary between tics, perseverations (excessive continuation of a specific motor or verbal behavior), and stereotypical behaviors (idiosyncratic repetition of a movement, also known in the field of autism as stimming) versus OCBs is often hard to specify. As alluded to in an earlier section, OCBs can also coexist with what may seem, at first glance, to be their polar opposites: impulsivities and ADHD.[85] For example, a child with a fear of getting hurt might, confusingly, manifest cutting behaviors. These problems seem best conceptualized as representing the real-life complexities of neurobiological dysregulation. Again, remember that, in actuality, the exact label is usually far less relevant than the treatment strategy. Consequently, the information and suggestions that are given in this book can be used without complete diagnostic certainty.

Children with Asperger's may also display repetitive body-focused behaviors (RBFBs). Although different from tics in some ways, these are a group of problems that also have both impulsive and compulsive aspects. Like tics, RBFBs can be triggered by stimuli ranging from excitement to boredom, or can just seem like really bad habits, which makes them very confusing to understand and address clinically.[86] The best-known RBFBs are compulsive hair pulling or twisting (trichotillomania), compulsive nail biting (onychophagia), and compulsive skin picking (dermatillomania).

Action for Parents

If this has been an issue, work on developing more perspective about tics or any other kind of RBFB being unintentional; also remember that expecting your child to stop just because you want them to is very unlikely to be helpful or to be experienced as reflecting either caring or support.

Obsessive-Compulsive Behaviors and School

It may come as no surprise that obsessive-compulsive behaviors can significantly affect a child's school adjustment in terms of grades, social relationships, and attitude toward learning. This list includes problems that may occur in school settings:

- Disappearing into the bathroom to repetitively hand wash

- Perfectionistic sharpening of pencils

- Having to shape letters perfectly

- Being unable to resist rereading sentences

- Having to be first in line

- Not being able to touch certain "gooey" classroom materials

- Avoiding being even lightly brushed by another student

- Obsessing about the same inappropriate subject

- Counting ceiling tiles, number of steps to the next class, or syllables or designated letters (e.g., how many Ls) in the teacher's verbalizations

Providing psychoeducational materials to the school, teacher conferences, and developing formal or informal accommodations are just some approaches to OCBs in educational environments. Although OCBs and obsessive-compulsive disorder are by far better known than they were in the past, there are still many educators who have never had a student with these issues. Understanding and valuing how parents and the educational team can partner is an essential part of ensuring any child's progress.

It is important to bear in mind that OCBs frequently turn virtues into vices. In high-functioning children with Asperger's, OCBs are sometimes manifested in extremely excessive studying that can present quite a dilemma to both parents and teachers. In general, compulsive studying is ultimately self-defeating; those who engage in this practice will rarely develop long-term life balance or healthy social-emotional functioning, even if they achieve financial success.

Action for Parents

Find out whether OCBs are a problem in school. Also, reflect on whether the present approach to grades, homework, and studying is promoting a balanced life and a calm, happy home environment.

The Importance of Early Intervention

Why are obsessive-compulsive behaviors so important to address early and effectively for children with Asperger's syndrome? Here's why:

- OCBs make it harder to teach essential communication and social skills, and may interfere with academic progress.

- OCBs reinforce self-centeredness and reduce opportunities for positive social interactions. For example, children who express the urge to bounce anything they touch will be paying little attention to the people around them.

- OCBs are an obstacle to social growth because they contribute to the atypical social presentation that is already a problem for children with AS. Compulsively talking about weather-related events, or playing card games that no one else is interested in, is hardly the way to foster good relationships.

There is another powerful reason to address OCBs as early as possible: These behaviors have a strong possibility of increasing over time. Why? Because the "solution" of reducing discomfort via a ritual is very temporary and, in the long run, would more than likely result in an increase in OCBs (remember the discussion in a previous section about how negative reinforcement works). Therefore, engaging in a compulsion or getting reassurance presents the same problem as giving candy to a child who is having a tantrum. Would you expect that child to have more or fewer tantrums in the future? Of course, the answer is more. Responding to a child's repetitive questions may temporarily provide relief but will only reinforce the need for compulsive questioning in the future, and the same process would hold true for any other compulsions. As OCD progresses, those affected often lose the sense of control over their own thought processes, and their ability to prioritize life tasks degrades. For example, to a seriously impaired man, shaving perfectly may appear equally as important as getting to his job on time. All too often, commitment to seeking the necessary help occurs only when matters have reached crisis level.

 Action for Parents

Consider whether the level of services being received is adequate to truly address your child's present needs.

Takeaway Action

This is the time when you can start really building your foundation of knowledge. Reflect on at least three facts or concepts in the preceding section that made a particular impression on you.

Section III
Treating Obsessive-Compulsive Behaviors in Children with Asperger's Syndrome

Ready for some good news? In many areas there are more professionals knowledgeable about the diagnosis and treatment of obsessive-compulsive behaviors and Asperger's syndrome than would have been the case even a relatively few years ago. However, for many parents, accessing the most effective clinical and educational team for their child can still be somewhat confusing and frustrating, as many places continue to lack professionals with the needed expertise.

Parents in some countries might find that there are minimal resources to address their child's needs regarding treatment of OCBs. If feasible, sometimes it is appropriate to travel to a country where proper evaluation and treatment is available. If not, some centers are exploring teleconferencing options or perhaps will have scholarships for those in need. Very resourceful parents might consider organizing a conference or society that can bring the experts to them. Sadly, there are many parents who do not have the means to realistically consider these alternatives, and an answer to their circumstances is simply not available.

What kind of practitioner should be consulted first? How do parents know whether the professionals evaluating or treating their child have the right training, or have enough experience? What's more important: the rapport that exists with the therapist or the therapist's level of skills? These are not easy questions for parents to address. Some reasonable steps are to ask the present medical doctors, contact local university or hospital-based specialized treatment programs, or attend local support groups and ask other parents for resources and directions they have found useful. Not-for-profit foundations can often provide lists of names, but their bylaws may prohibit them from telling what they really think about specific practitioners. Searching the Internet can be a mixed blessing—it's hard to separate legitimate from dubious websites—and the same is true of advertisements. Asking an insurance company for referrals can have an unpredictable outcome; they may point parents in the right direction, but they may know only what the practitioners who are enrolled with them have stated about themselves.

Probably, in the final analysis, there is going to be no real substitute for parents using their own diligence and common sense and doing their own evaluations in comparing what any given practitioner is recommending versus what they have learned to be sensible and evidence-based courses of action and recommendations. For instance, if the practitioner suggests very general play therapy as a treatment for OCBs, or suggests saturating children with reassurances until they are totally convinced they are safe and secure, or believes that OCBs are a response to a child's unconscious conflicts stemming from deficient parenting skills, it may be wise to seek other opinions.

Action for Parents
Read articles and additional books that discuss evidence-based approaches to OCBs.

Readiness for Change

One of the most important factors to consider in any intervention plan is the readiness for change. In many areas of behavioral science, it has been shown that treatment is more likely to be successful if readiness for change is high. Further, interventions are more likely to work if they are matched to level of readiness. Readiness for change has been described as a series of steps progressing from denial and minimization to taking action and maintaining gains over time.[87] There are questionnaires that assess readiness for change that can be tailored ad hoc to assess the problem of obsessive-compulsive behaviors in the context of Asperger's syndrome; these may be part of the assessment process for certain children. However, developing a general sense of the child's readiness for change may also take place more informally, via discussions about this subject with the child or from behavioral observations.

Learning how to listen and support "change talk" about their OCBs from a child with AS is a great parenting skill. For example, if the child says, "I'm sick of having to wear the same color shirt over and over," an attentive parent could reflect back the potential desire for change that this statement might indicate by saying something like, "I guess you might be thinking about whether you could challenge yourself by trying to wear a shirt with different colors."

Clearly, readiness for changing OCBs is likely to be low for a lot of children with AS. Fortunately, there are strategies that can be used to address this obstacle. These include capitalizing on even small amounts of distress or inconvenience from their OCBs, on their desire to fit in better socially, or on their motivation to earn a reward or work toward a goal.

When children's readiness for change is so low that only external pressure is an option, their parents' readiness for change becomes even more important. For parents faced with this situation, readiness means:

- Realizing the need to separate their own readiness for change from that of their child

- Being realistic about the problems associated with their child's OCBs remaining the same or worsening

- Truly understanding how improving OCBs will benefit functioning and quality of life for the entire family

- Maintaining commitment to the best plan for their child, even through all the roadblocks

Action for Parents

Attend closely to and support any verbal or nonverbal signs from your child that they have even the slightest readiness to challenge their OCBs.

Initial Consultations

Addressing obsessive-compulsive behaviors in children with Asperger's syndrome requires knowledge, practice, and a whole lot of patience. The best intervention plans are comprehensive but also tailored to the individualized needs of each child, so the level of intensity required to maximize treatment gains is best considered on a case-by-case basis. The beginning of OCB treatment can make or break a successful course of treatment, so this period of time will be discussed in some detail.

Prior to meeting with a clinician—a physician, psychologist, or other kind of allied health professional—parents are generally asked to fill out a variety of informational and assessment forms. They may be provided with some educational or orientation reading material. These steps have several purposes: to establish a record of background and contact information; to provide parents with an understanding of how the clinical practice operates; to fill them in about important matters such as HIPAA regulations, including confidentiality of records; and to advise them on what to do if there is a need for emergency intervention or, less urgently, a change in appointment schedule. By law, treatment of a minor can take place only with written parental consent.

For those parents seeking specialized professional assistance, it all starts with making sure they, and if feasible, their child, understand what is meant by the term obsessive-compulsive behavior. Some come to their first session with clarity about this, but many have never discussed this matter before with a clinician. (Parents who have read this book will presumably be among those who enter treatment with at least a basic level of understanding of OCBs and, hopefully, quite a bit more.)

There are parents who come to the first session alone, and others who want their child to participate in whatever manner the child is capable of from the outset. In many instances, very seasoned and specialized clinicians may provide examples and anecdotes about OCBs, often from their own practice experiences, but with identifying details disguised enough to preserve confidentiality. This is done to help increase understanding and further show that the OCBs being discussed are far from uncommon (although even the most highly experienced practitioners occasionally encounter those "never seen it before" cases that require more thought and investigation than usual).

Initial consultations are important as they often set the tone for what follows, including whether there is a meeting of the minds among the parents, the clinician, and the child; whether a trusting therapeutic relationship can be established; and whether treatment begins in a focused, goal-directed manner. Therefore, it is important for parents to understand what needs to take place in an effective initial consultation process. Other than obtaining information about OCBs, the first consultation can include the following:

- *Review of past records.* It's a good idea to bring copies of the child's past evaluations and school history to the initial meeting.

- *Ascertaining the child's developmental and medical history.* This helps clinicians have a context for how the child is functioning at the present time, his or her path toward the time of the initial consultation, and whether there are any physiological issues that need to be taken into consideration (e.g., using treatment strategies that generate a high level of anxiety, albeit temporarily, in a child who has asthma).

- *Obtaining a basic family history of medical, neurological, psychological, and developmental issues in close genetic relatives.* While genetics is not exactly destiny, it does help to be aware of the presence of any significant familial difficulties that might bear upon the diagnosis or prognosis (e.g., whether there are any family members who have tics).

- *Examining whether there are any co-occurring psychological, neurological, or learning disorders.* It is important to be aware of coexisting conditions as they might affect how treatment is sequenced (e.g., if a child is very depressed, it is important to address this early in treatment) or presented (e.g., giving assignments that require reading would not be appropriate if the child has a deficit in this skill).

- *Understanding the family structure.* Knowing whether a child has siblings and the nature of their relationship can help the clinician design the treatment plan as effectively as possible. Imagine the difference between implementing a treatment plan when there is a provocative older brother who calls the child affected by AS/OCBs "weirdo" versus implementing the same plan when the brother is supportive and encouraging. It is also helpful to have some information about parental work situations. For example, knowing that one parent is often away from home on business trips, leaving the other parent to manage the child with AS plus two other children, will surely affect the way between-session assignments are given and how lack of follow-through, if this occurs, is discussed.

- *Developing an initial treatment plan.* Parents are well advised to consider treatment plans (especially beginning ones) dynamic and flexible, yet all treatment plans have to start somewhere. By the end of the initial consultation process, there will ideally be some agreement about the goals of the early stages of treatment, an outline of the strategies that will be used, who is responsible for doing what, how progress will be measured and reported, and a provisional overview of the entire treatment plan.

- *Making referrals for additional needed assessments.* It is not uncommon to seek the perspectives of a number of practitioners in different specialties (e.g., medical/neurological examination, psychological testing). What is needed in this regard is often discussed during the initial consultation process.

- *Obtaining written releases.* Patient confidentiality is protected legally and taken very seriously by licensed clinicians. No information about a child's prior treatments can be obtained without a parent's (or a designated legal guardian's) written authorization. Similarly, no records or other kinds of communication can be provided to other parties without the parent's or legal guardian's consent.

- *Responding to any questions or concerns about the treatment process.* Not only is it appropriate to ask questions and clarify parents' (or the child's) concerns with behavioral and mental health practitioners, it is also advisable. Having numerous questions is the norm rather than the exception when it comes to the field of behavioral and mental health. Parents have sought out a practitioner because they are looking for answers, so they should ask their questions without hesitation.

These segments often take place in a single meeting although sometimes there is need for an extended consultation that takes place over two or more meetings.

Identifying Specific Obsessive-Compulsive Behaviors

The next matter to address is, what obsessive-compulsive behaviors are involved? Producing a list of the child's OCBs that is as thorough as possible is necessary for effective intervention. Information can be gathered from parents, teachers, and any other person who is likely to have good knowledge of the child's behaviors. The reason to get data from multiple sources is that children will often manifest different OCBs as situations vary (e.g., in school versus at home) and as a function of their differing relationships (e.g., in front of their mothers as opposed to their fathers).

Interviewing the child is also very important, although some children cannot or will not be responsive. The accuracy of data gained in this interview will vary from child to child, according to their functional levels, verbal skills, and ability or desire to convey information about their OCBs. It is important for the interviewer to have a good rapport with the child and to ask questions that are very specific; questions that are open-ended are not likely to yield data that is meaningful for creating an effective treatment plan. For example, if it has been reported that the child has bedtime rituals, it is more useful to inquire about the specific bedtime behaviors that are typical regarding OCBs than to ask, "What do you do at bedtime?" It is also essential to establish what aspects of the OCBs make a child feel temporarily better, or at least not worse (remember the earlier discussion about functionality). These behaviors will often become the ones the child practices refraining from in order to make progress. Often, the most important information the clinician will gather is about what "benefit" children get from their OCBs.

Some instruments initially developed for obsessive-compulsive disorder can help clinicians further a good working understanding of a child's OCBs. One of these measures is the Children's Yale-Brown OC Scale (CY-BOCS).[88] This instrument is administered by clinicians and yields a score that indicates the present severity of the child's obsessive-compulsive symptoms. It also includes an extensive self-report symptom checklist. Another measure that may be used is the Leyton Obsessional Inventory-Child Version (LOI-CV).[89] However, it should be kept in mind that neither of these tests was specifically designed for assessing children with Asperger's syndrome.

Action for Parents

If you've already identified some OCBs, rank them according to your perception of most to least troublesome.

Psychoeducation

If a mutual agreement can be reached between the parents, clinician, and ideally the child about the basic goals and purpose of treatment and the manner in which it will progress, further psychoeducation can proceed. Psychoeducation concerns defining basic terms (e.g., what an OCB is) and also describing the rationale for the clinical plan. Whether the treatment will be done by the intake clinician, by another colleague, or by a team of practitioners may be addressed. In actual practice, ongoing psychoeducation, and frequently the restating of specific concepts, perhaps using different illustrating examples, occurs throughout the therapeutic process. In the absence of agreement on goals and methodologies, treatment often stalls or is possibly discontinued by either parents or the therapist. Sometimes it helps to get a second or even a third opinion. There are many instances when parents terminate therapy and later reconsider. Most therapists will accept this as fairly typical, and there is no reason for parents to feel reluctant or embarrassed to contact a particular therapist again.

The psychoeducational session is a good time for parents, and ideally the child, to ask questions and verbalize their concerns, and there can be many. Therapeutic concepts should be explained and, hopefully, accepted; the pros and cons of alternative approaches need to be explored. For example, parents often have particular worries about exposure-based therapies (further discussed below) as they can trigger an escalation of distress or negative, even aggressive behaviors known, somewhat euphemistically as "response bursts." Giving parents the understanding, confidence, and strategies to cope with response bursts is particularly relevant at the outset of treatment, when this kind of reaction is most likely to occur. If an externalizing concept (like thinking of OCBs as a mad scientist trying to get a child to believe his wacky ideas) is going to be used, it is explained at this point. Boosting both the child's and parents' motivational levels is part and parcel of this early phase of treatment, although for many children with AS and OCBs, it is the parents' attitude that is paramount.

Action for Parents
If there is anything about the proposed treatment plan that does not make sense to you, make sure to communicate this to the relevant practitioner.

Next Steps

As a prelude to the active phase of treatment, the therapist may have the child draw pictures related to his or her obsessive-compulsive behaviors; these pictures can include those of the child "fighting back." (As treatment continues, this exercise can be repeated at various times with the drawings serving as a talking point for discussing, and assessing, progress or other therapeutic matters.) This visual connection is especially relevant for children with Asperger's syndrome, who are often visual learners.[90] There are many creative activities and games that can increase rapport and help bond the child and the therapist in a common purpose to work together to defeat OCBs. For example, practicing talking back to an OCB can be a constructive role-playing exercise; this can also be done using brief social stories or comic strips. For instance, the child can make up a story that involves sitting in a nonpreferred chair or traveling to school via a different route and coping effectively with the discomfort these challenges entail.

Often, the next step is working to create a hierarchy of target OCBs to address. The hierarchy may consist of breaking down one OCB into small steps or may include a variety of OCBs. However, specifying too many behaviors to work on at once is counterproductive. The idea is to rate the items in the hierarchy in terms of how much distress they are associated with. If the child is able to adequately comprehend the SUDS concept, which is typically used for this purpose, so much the better. SUDS stands for Subjective Units of Distress Scale. Simply put, the child is asked to rate each item from 1 to 10, with 10 denoting the most distress. Some children cannot do these ratings; perhaps they do not have actual comprehension of the task, lack the facility with language, or are too perfectionistic to risk providing a rating that is not 100% true. For these children, the parents can help with the rating; a behavioral avoidance test can be done (the more the avoidance or apparent distress, the higher the rating); or nonverbal approaches (e.g., pictures) can be tried. However, especially in the case of younger or lower-functioning children, there are times when therapists just have to rely on their experience, make educated guesses, and learn how to proceed by trial and error. If your child's therapist does not create a hierarchy of OCBs, it could mean that they lack specialized experience, or that they are so expert they basically know how to proceed without doing this in such a formal way.

Next comes the actual intervention phase. Parents should realistically expect that treatment plans for OCBs almost never proceed according to schedule and that ongoing troubleshooting and problem solving is par for the course. As a famous military dictum states, the initial battle plan lasts until the first engagement with the enemy. Obsessive-compulsive behaviors can wax and wane in ways that at times defy explanation, and progress, or lack of progress, needs to be continuously monitored. Therefore, parents are well advised to not overreact to great days or really bad days. When it comes to OCBs, consistency, patience, emotional stability, and resilience are excellent watchwords to internalize and live by.

One can find many kinds of interventions for obsessive-compulsive disorder that cover the gamut from evidence-based to highly speculative. Consequently, it is important to be practical, realistic, and an educated consumer when evaluating treatment options. If some practitioner, merchant, or advertisement promises a cure, particularly a quick and easy one, parents may wish to seriously consider running in the other direction. Unfortunately, there is no known cure, no easy answer, no magic bullet for OCD or OCBs. This is particularly the case for extraordinarily severe, treatment-resistant (refractory) cases. In these thankfully rare instances, investigative interventions such as psychosurgery[91] or deep brain stimulation[92] are sometimes the treatments of last resort.

On a more positive note, however, there are strategies that can help when properly and consistently implemented. The two kinds of interventions that have the strongest evidence-based support at present are cognitive behavioral therapy and medication.[93]

Overview of Cognitive Behavioral Therapy

Cognitive behavioral therapy (CBT) may be thought of as a group of ideas and methods that directly seek to modify problem behaviors and cognitions (thoughts). It is among the most widely used and research-supported form of psychotherapy, with roots in both the Stoic philosophy of the ancient Greeks that emphasized the importance of rational, constructive, nonreactive thinking, and modern learning theory.

Cognitive behavioral therapy is differentiated from many other forms of psychotherapy because of its emphasis on problem solving in the present (rather than on past events) and its suitability to be used in a scientific framework and verified through research.

Cognitive behavioral therapy has been documented to be effective with both children and adults. It has been applied to psychological conditions like anxiety disorders, obsessive-compulsive disorder, mood disorders, autism, and Tourette's syndrome, to name a few. It has also been helpful in interpersonal and marital issues, health problems such as stress, and enhancing performance in sports, academics, and work. Pediatric application of CBT can be a powerful tool to help children. Restructuring thinking patterns and changing behavior at an early age can lead to healthier and more functional coping mechanisms for life, especially for children at higher risk for developing emotional and behavioral problems.

A substantial body of research indicates that altering behavior or thoughts directly often leads to improvements. Further, there is growing proof that modifying thoughts and behaviors can affect neurological processes similar to the way meditation, yoga, therapeutic massage, or aerobic exercise can benefit a physiological measure like blood pressure.[94] One of the most important recent understandings in the field of brain science is that the brain is more modifiable, or neuroplastic, than previously imagined. Some may be concerned that CBT is like a Band-Aid, meaning that treatment without uncovering "deeper" causes is superficial. Fortunately for those considering CBT, there is little evidence that this is true. A related form of therapy that appears promising to many is acceptance and commitment therapy, commonly known as ACT,[95] which highlights a high level of tolerance for internal sensations and cognitions and emphasizes the referencing of one's choices to a positive value system. Similarly, the motivational interviewing (MI) approach can be used in conjunction with CBT by finding ways to decrease existing mind-sets that impede change, and enhancing thoughts and behaviors that can move the child in a positive direction.[96] The "change talk" previously referred to is a focus of the MI approach.

Although cognitive and behavior therapy are often used jointly, the following sections examine each of the treatment types separately.

Cognitive Therapy

Cognitive therapy[97] starts with the notion that many kinds of psychological problems are related to habitual errors in thinking; for example, magnification of minor problems into major issues, taking negative comments from others personally, and jumping to conclusions without sufficient evidence. It has been found that problems such as depression, anxiety, and anger, as well as a host of others, have characteristic erroneous schemas (habitual belief systems). In cognitive therapy, such errors are identified and then challenged and restructured through mental exercises that are taught and practiced during and between sessions. The good news is that research shows that correcting faulty schemas can greatly help a variety of symptoms and problems and lead to lasting positive changes in overall functioning and quality of life.

Action for Parents

Recall two instances when making constructive changes in your own thinking helped you feel better or cope more effectively with a challenging problem.

Cognitive Restructuring in Obsessive-Compulsive Disorder

Cognitive restructuring is a CBT method that has been usefully applied to obsessive-compulsive disorder, based upon the work of investigators such as Dr. Paul Salkovskis and Dr. Paul Emmelkamp, among others.[98] The idea in this strategy is to learn how to modify habitual thinking errors common in OCD. It is thought that challenging these faulty ideas can lead to reduction in OCD behaviors. These errors in thinking include:[99]

- *Inflated sense of responsibility.* One example would be a boy who believes that the health of his mother, or of Planet Earth, is entirely his responsibility.

- *Overimportance of thoughts/importance of controlling thoughts.* Children with OCD often have a faulty belief that the process of thinking is of paramount importance and that they should be able to control what they think. This is why they can become so guilt-ridden and self-critical even if they have not done anything wrong in reality. They fail to recognize that thinking per se is an involuntary process and exists independently of behavior. As proof, first see how long you can go without thinking anything at all, then move your arm while thinking "Arm, don't move."

- *Needing guarantees and certainty.* Errors of this kind occur in children who have to know answers "for sure"; 99% certainty is just not good enough for them.

- *Having to be perfect.* For children who manifest this cognitive error, there is an absolute right way and wrong way to think or behave; in other words, no gray areas. They believe that perfect actions are the only ones that count.

- *Overestimating the probability of harm.* A minor threat to well-being is magnified out of all proportion for children showing this type of cognitive error; for instance, that a sore throat indicates a life-threatening illness, or that a single bad grade in middle school will result in homelessness.

- *Equating thoughts with behaviors.* This is also known as thought-action fusion. In a magical way, thinking a negative thought about someone else can hurt that individual in reality.

These kinds of errors result in the misunderstandings and misappraisals that are common in OCD and that are hypothesized to result in "neutralizing" (i.e., compulsions or avoidance behaviors). Sometimes these errors are codified over time into flawed schemas, or maladaptive organizing concepts, that guide a child's life. An example of a self-defeating schema that a child with OCD might develop would be: "I can't trust anyone, including myself."

The process of cognitive restructuring for OCD involves (1) becoming more aware of the core issues in one's faulty, inaccurate thinking; (2) actively challenging the veracity of this thinking; and (3) replacing erroneous cognitions with more accurate and helpful anti-OCD beliefs.[100] The benefits of making these kinds of changes in self-talk have been found to work quite automatically; oddly enough, people don't even have to truly believe what they are saying in their own minds for this method to help. Imagine you were doing push-ups every day while telling yourself, "This won't make me stronger." You'd gain strength anyway, wouldn't you?

Action for Parents
Practice observing cognitive errors in the ongoing way a difficulty is expressed verbally or handled behaviorally.

Rational Emotive Behavior Therapy

The late Dr. Albert Ellis developed a very useful research-based model of cognitive therapy, called rational emotive (behavior) therapy or REBT.[101] The structured nature of REBT particularly lends itself to being tailored to address OCBs in children with Asperger's syndrome but only for those with adequately developed verbal skills. Using REBT should not be equated with rationalizing poor behavior or justifying not taking responsibility for one's actions; in fact, when used properly, REBT accomplishes just the reverse. Here are the basics, presented in Ellis's classic ABCDEF model:

A. First, consider the situation or Activating Event.

B. Next, there are the Irrational/Erroneous Beliefs. These are the upsetting, erroneous, or otherwise maladaptive thoughts, perceptions, and schemas about what occurred at point A.

C. This point is where unhelpful, excessive, self-defeating emotional and behavioral reactions, or Consequences, occur.

D. Disputing follows; there is an active attempt to refute the faulty cognitions that took place at point B and led to the problematic feelings and behaviors at point C. The disputing process is similar to what a lawyer would do to challenge evidence that is lacking in a factual basis. The lawyer would ask, "Where is the evidence?"

E. The goal at point E is to construct a More Effective Philosophy, one that both accepts the realities of life and promotes adaptive reasoning and emotions.

F. The hope is that by going from A to E, a new set of Less Debilitating Feelings can lastingly emerge.

Most people erroneously believe that situations instead of their thoughts are the cause of their feelings and behaviors. The key corrective concept to learn in this form of cognitive restructuring is that the A is often not the fundamental problem; it's the B that is the most helpful area to focus upon. That is to say, it's not what happens to us that is the root cause of how we feel and behave; to the contrary, it's about our perceptions and processing of what has happened. Of course, in real life there are frequently multiple As, Bs, and Cs that need to be addressed.

Let's work through an example of REBT involving a child who becomes angry and tantrums after being told that TV time is over and it's bedtime.

A. (Activating Event): Being told to turn off the TV and get ready for bed.

B. (Irrational/Erroneous Beliefs): "I should not be told to turn off the TV and go to bed."

C. (Consequences): Angry feelings and oppositional-defiant behaviors; for example, "I'm mad and I will keep turning on the TV and running away if you try to get me to go to my room."

D. (Disputing): "Where is there a law that says my parents have to say the things I want them to?" or "Who ever said that I am in charge of the TV?"

E. (More Effective Philosophy): "OK, even though I always want to be in control, this is not the way life really works; life is about give-and-take."

F. (Less Debilitating Feelings): Anger dissipates totally or is experienced in a milder form as annoyance; the behaviors that reflect anger are lessened.

This scenario sounds like it would be too good to be true, but many children with AS and OCBs can actually learn how to do this with enough practice. And would it hurt their parents to use this technique too?

Action for Parents
Come up with an example using the ABCDEF formula to address a parenting dilemma. This can be done in your head, but it's usually more helpful to specifically write down each step, especially when first learning to use this technique.

Anger Management

Children with Asperger's often experience and express dysregulated anger (i.e., too much or too little, at the wrong time, or in the wrong situation).[102] Learning anger management strategies goes hand in hand with assertiveness training, which is discussed later. Cognitively, anger is related to having unrealistic "rules" and expectations regarding other people and situations (e.g., "Other children should always be nice to me"). The idea is to learn how to change anger-creating "shoulds, oughts, and musts" into more reasonable preferences and wishes combined with positive coping statements (e.g., "It would be great if other kids were always nice to me, but it's not the end of the world if they're not"). It works even better if the child learns how to add on a self-statement that enhances coping (e.g., "When they're not nice to me, I can always try to find someone else to play with or do something fun on my own"). And when awareness of anger triggers and the ability to moderate the physical aspects of anger (e.g., clenched fists, tightened facial muscles) are developed, anger management can be improved even further. Since excessive anger can interfere with therapeutic interventions, it is imperative that children with AS receiving treatment for OCBs learn the skills to modulate this mood.

Action for Parents
Listen for the "shoulds" the next time your child expresses anger. (It might be a good idea to pay attention to the unhelpful "shoulds" in your own parenting style too!)

Behavior Therapy

Behavior therapy is the term used to describe a variety of strategies designed to increase positive behaviors and decrease negative ones. This approach emphasizes objective goals that can be measured and observed (e.g., increasing the number of social interactions that last more than five minutes) rather than subjective abstractions (e.g., becoming happier). Behavior therapy examines the functional relationships between stimuli that occur prior to the target behavior (antecedents) and how the behavior is reinforced or punished (consequences); for example, examining what changes take place when a parent ceases attending to mild negative behaviors and starts ignoring them. Understanding these relationships via data collection leads to a theory about how the problem behavior was acquired and why it is persisting. The end product is implementation of an intervention plan to modify the undesirable behavior. A major advantage of behavior therapy is that progress may be charted in an immediately useful manner.

Action for Parents

As an experiment, select a behavior that you desire to see decrease, like whining, and see what happens if you ignore every instance of it for two weeks.

Exposure and Response Prevention

The most effective, well-researched cognitive behavioral strategy for classic OCD is called exposure and response prevention (ERP; also known as exposure and ritual prevention).[103] Here's an example: Let's suppose a ten-year-old boy has developed a ritual that involves having to hit his own head if he has an upsetting or "unlucky" thought. He would be asked to gradually learn to have upsetting thoughts on purpose (exposure) and to refrain from hitting his head (response prevention). At first, he would likely feel quite a bit of discomfort, but as time passed his discomfort would be expected to lessen and eventually dissipate. With enough practice, this ritual could eventually be extinguished altogether.

This biologically based process of an individual's learning, with protracted experience, to become less uncomfortable with distressing stimuli is called habituation.[104] The basic concept is that compulsions (and avoidant behaviors) are like tricks used to reduce the discomfort of obsessions (or unpleasant bodily sensations). Remember, these tricks actually can provide relief, but usually only briefly. Over time, more tricks may be needed to achieve relief, and the relief may become ever more fleeting, often resulting in a vicious cycle of worsening.

Exposure and response prevention is typically conducted according to a hierarchy in which less distressing symptoms are tackled first, with progress up the ladder of discomfort proceeding according to the child's feedback. The child is taught to give the clinician subjective ratings (e.g., 1 to 10, with 10 being the most distressing) regarding readiness for challenging OCD symptoms. With very young children, the hierarchy may be more reflective of the perceptions of the parents and clinical judgment of the therapist.

This approach seems to work best when it is done in situations that closely approximate what occurs in the individual's regular life. Especially for children with Asperger's syndrome, just talking about or imagining that they are challenging their discomforts would not suffice, although this can be a good first step. So if a child has an OCB about driving along a certain path to school, the ideal is to work up to practicing the challenge of going a different way.

Because there is an initial period of heightened discomfort or anxiety, the whole concept of ERP at first glance seems to go against the natural instincts of parents and caregivers. What caregiver wants to cause a child distress, particularly a child who is already experiencing problems? It's helpful to think of ERP as being similar to undergoing dental work: unpleasant and expensive in the short run but surely better than the physical and financial distress that would be experienced if teeth or gums deteriorate.

The method may also appear odd and even perhaps unloving or cruel to some well-intentioned relatives or friends. These folks may try to talk parents out of attempting this kind of intervention or to sabotage the efforts of the parents or treatment team. For example, a grandfather who simply cannot tolerate seeing his grandchild upset might ignore a request to cease answering repetitive questions about whether it is going to rain or to stop buying model trucks. Providing explanatory readings or websites or inviting the relative or friend to a support group or even a treatment session may help. However, sometimes the situation is so bad that parents have no choice but to tell these relatives or friends that they cannot be around the child during some phases of active treatment.

Assertiveness Training

Advocating for themselves by communicating effectively, both verbally and nonverbally, is a characteristic problem for those with Asperger's. Assertiveness training teaches them the importance of expressing oneself in a manner that respects both others and self and how to differentiate passive, aggressive, and assertive communication. Identifying erroneous thinking that results in nonassertiveness and rehearsing assertive self-expression are key aspects of this training. Learning to be more assertive comes in handy for children with AS in gaining skills to hold their ground against OCBs.

Habit Reversal Training

Habit reversal training[105] (HRT) is often a good choice for addressing the tics and repetitive body-focused behaviors that often occur alongside OCBs. This package of strategies includes awareness training and learning replacement behaviors that compete with the problem behaviors. For example, holding one's arms stiffly with closed fists might be learned as a competing behavior for the urge to pull out one's hair. For any child, let alone one with Asperger's, learning to use HRT well takes a lot of motivation, patience, and self-discipline. Realistically, only certain children with AS will be able to use HRT effectively.

Social Skills Training

Social skills training (SST) comprises a group of strategies that are potentially helpful with OCBs.[106] The training includes instruction in maintaining the proper physical social distance, taking turns in a conversation, sharing possessions, and having knowledge about a diversity of topics. The basic idea is that by enhancing social functioning, more opportunities for challenging OCBs will naturally occur, and a virtuous cycle can develop in the following manner: Becoming more socially aware and wanting to have more positive social relationships can enhance motivation to control OCBs; controlling OCBs, in turn, can help improve interpersonal relationships.

Progressive Muscle Relaxation

Progressive muscle relaxation (PMR) is the systematic tensing and releasing of various muscle groups to increase awareness of somatic bracing (unnecessary tightness) that may contribute to the child's level

115

of anxiety and contribute to increasing OCBs.[107] This is a very well-researched method that can have lasting benefits—both medical (e.g., lowered blood pressure) and psychological (e.g., increased sense of well-being)—when practiced regularly. One caveat: PMR should not be used during exposure therapy implementation as it can interfere with the habituation process. This approach should also be carefully considered before using it with someone experiencing or prone to psychosis, as it can make one's cognitive set feel "looser." Similarly, in some instances PMR can engender sensations that can trigger or mimic panic attacks.

Family Therapy

Family therapy is an important modality to help teach everyone in the family who is old enough, or capable of learning, how to best support the fight against OCBs. In this therapy, roles, goals, and "loopholes" that the child with Asperger's might try to slide by with can be thoroughly discussed. Often there are concerns and issues among family members about how to challenge OCBs that they have never before verbalized. For children with OCBs, the value of knowing that they have their family's understanding and support cannot be overestimated.

Home Behavior Plans

Reducing OCBs both directly, by implementing specific therapeutic CBT strategies in the child's home setting, and indirectly, by helping foster a positive and constructive home culture, is the focus of home behavior plans. They can additionally support generalization from other treatment settings to the home environment, often where the highest level of OCBs exists.

Formulating a constructive and acceptable home behavior plan requires considerable effort; most important is the consistency and patience of the parents over time. The exigencies of daily life can easily lead to rationalizing counter-therapeutic exceptions as denoting flexibility and understanding (e.g., "It's his birthday, so let's not be hard on him today"); in reality, exceptions give children mixed messages and undermine their accountability. One caveat: A home behavior plan that has too many time-consuming and complicated elements (like very detailed charting requirements) is less likely to be feasible to use over time. When the plan is too arduous, initial enthusiasm tends to fade all too quickly as intervention fatigue increases.

Modifying Cognitive Behavioral Therapy for Obsessive-Compulsive Behaviors in Children with Asperger's Syndrome

How can these strategies, especially cognitive behavioral therapy, realistically be brought into play to help address the problem of obsessive-compulsive behaviors in Asperger's syndrome? Understandably, many parents ask this question.

Here is just one example: Some years ago, E. Katia Moritz, Ph.D., my colleague at the NeuroBehavioral Institute, wrote a children's book called Blink, Blink, Clop, Clop: Why Do We Do Things We Can't Stop? Recently reimagined as Blink, Blink, Clop, Clop: An OCD Storybook, the book translates CBT concepts about OCD into reading material with simple explanations that are understandable and fun for children, especially those with AS.[108] Dr. Moritz created a character called OC Flea, a bullying bug that tries to get a group of animals to engage in obsessive-compulsive behaviors. In the book, a wise owl educates the animals about how to fight back against OC Flea. This idea led to the development of various creative forms, games, and activities that teach children strategies to fight OCD. Although the book was originally designed for more classic forms of OCD, since its original publication many children with Asperger's syndrome have learned how to fight their own OC Fleas; for example, children may think of the flea as bullying them to repeat movie dialogue perfectly. Over the years, many parents have also learned how to use the OC Flea concept to help their children fight their OCBs. However, some older children may feel that the OC Flea concept is too babyish and will often prefer to learn the "real" terminology.

As often takes place in real life, many of these children may struggle to understand OCD is actually a bully and not their friend- especially at first. Although much easier said than done, useful concepts to address bullying from OCBs in Asperger's include:

- Sometimes just ignoring a bully works, but if the bully is causing a situation that is seriously affecting a child's feelings or involves a dangerous situation—for example, creating an urge to walk across a street with closed eyes—then ignoring is not the proper technique.

- Bullies rely on their targets to stay silent, so children should not keep what a bully does secret. Instead, they should tell an adult who could help.

- Children should maintain a sense of humor. It's more than OK to poke sarcastic fun at these thoughts; for example, "Yeah right, like I always have to start walking with my right foot first."

- When all else fails, a bully might even pretend to be a child's friend or protector. Children should be reminded not to fall for their tricks. Even if it's a slow process, they should keep trying to find ways of breaking free of a bully's power to influence or control them.

Of course, for children, or anyone else for that matter, standing up to a bully is not easy. In fact, their problem is likely to get worse, or at least to feel worse, before it gets better. But when parents consider what will happen if they let the bully win, what choice do they really have?

Action for Parents

Compliment your child for attempts to fight back against OCBs, no matter how small at first; express how proud you are of your child for making this effort.

Building Resilience

Increased resilience, the capacity to manage stress and bounce back, is a foundation for other more specific symptom- or problem-focused methods, including ERP. Here are a few naturalistic resilience-supporting activities parents might want to attempt. While children trying them may not be happy campers, parents should keep in mind that (1) tantrums and complaints are distressing but likely not lethal; and (2) Rome wasn't built in a day.

- At a store, select a longer line than usual to wait on.
- Purposely drive somewhere at a time when there will be traffic delays.
- Pick a restaurant with a long wait time.
- Go to a theme park at a busy time of year and resist getting a "fast pass."

Action for Parents

Try one of the resilience-building ideas given above, or come up with one of your own to do along with your child.

Medications for Obsessive-Compulsive Behaviors

Much more is known about the use of medications in treating obsessive-compulsive disorder than in treating obsessive-compulsive behaviors manifesting in Asperger's syndrome.

The first reasonably effective medications for OCD were based upon research that pointed to the neurotransmitter (brain chemical messenger) serotonin having something to do with this condition. Today, there are a variety of medications, mainly in the SSRI (selective serotonin reuptake inhibitor) family, commonly used in the treatment of OCD.[109] Since these medications may not be efficacious on their own in many cases, they are often combined with augmenting agents (e.g., antipsychotics, mood stabilizers) to boost their effects or to address comorbid conditions as well as concomitant symptoms like overvalued ideation (poor insight), agitation, or disordered moods. A brief description of these kinds of medications was presented in an earlier section.

According to the Expert Consensus Guidelines on treatment of OCD,[110] medications are often not considered to be a stand-alone, first-line approach. When OCD is extremely severe, it is typically thought that combining medication and CBT from the outset is appropriate; in cases of lesser severity, and especially with children, an adequate trial of CBT should be tried before medication is used. In actuality, the first in-tervention parents often receive is a prescription. Even more concerning, the often erroneous idea of waiting for the medication to work before trying CBT seems fairly commonplace in real-life practice.

When it comes to OCBs in AS, the medical community currently lacks the kind of research base that informs the use of medications in treating more classic OCD. Medications must be selected on the basis that OCBs are similar to OCD in many respects; therefore often the same medication approach is often used. Prescribers are often very cautious in their recommendations, given the unpredictable ways that some children with OCBs might respond to a given agent, as well as the desire to not expose developing children to untoward side effects. Parents who choose (or have no true choice due to the severity of their child's condition) to consent to the use of medication for the treatment of OCBs commonly have to be patient through various trials and flexible in regard to trying new medicinal approaches, especially if the initial benefits are not lasting.

Since there is neither clear consensus nor an extremely effective medication regimen for OCBs, research into developing new agents, or finding novel uses for older agents, is ongoing. [111]

Alternative Therapies

Parents of children with Asperger's syndrome might not want their chil-dren to take psychotropic medication in the first place or might become discouraged if it has resulted in troublesome side effects or hasn't worked. Instead, they may want to try alternative approaches. While this section focuses on obsessive-compulsive behaviors, the cautions raised would be applicable to the subject of alternative therapies for AS in general.

While having an open mind is generally a good idea, reasonable caution is important when considering alternative treatments for OCBs. Alternative therapies include hypnosis, special dietary regimens, megavitamins and other dietary supplements, and hyperbaric chambers. Parents should be especially wary of red flags, such as suppliers who state that they are the only ones who know their method, that organized medicine is trying to suppress their findings, or that their techniques are too complicated to be systematically researched. Wise parents will carefully assess an alternative therapy before initiating it for their child. A problem in assessing these therapies is that much of their support seems to be anecdotal, rather than based on well-designed and objectively reviewed studies. This makes them highly susceptible to placebo effects, misattributions of natural variations in symptom levels, and wishful thinking. Remember, if it sounds too good to be true, it probably is. Nothing here should be interpreted to mean that the benefits of a healthy, nutritious diet and adequate exercise are being minimized—quite the opposite in fact.

Action for Parents

If your child's plan includes using an alternative treatment, ask the practitioner for some independent references regarding its scientific evidence base.

Obsessive-Compulsive Behaviors: Treatment Complexities

Once again, it is one thing to treat classic obsessive-compulsive disorder (difficult in its own right) and another to address obsessive-compulsive behaviors in children with Asperger's syndrome. But recognizing that a task might be very difficult is not the same as saying that it is hopeless. Applying and tailoring cognitive behavioral therapy concepts that were developed for children with classic OCD to OCBs co-occurring with autistic spectrum conditions has numerous challenges, obstacles, and complexities that would be disingenuous to minimize. Some of these are discussed in the following sections.

Less Available Research

In recent years, research about classic OCD has burgeoned.[112] The same, however, is not true insofar as OCBs in Asperger's are concerned, although a few studies are emerging.[113] Therefore, any statements regarding the proper protocol as well as effectiveness of treatments must be made cautiously at the present time. To date, there is no perfect, evidence-based anti-OCB approach for children with AS. It is hoped that more research in this area will be done as time goes by.

Intrinsic Characteristics of Asperger's Syndrome

The very nature of Asperger's interferes with treatment efforts. Learning therapeutic strategies is facilitated by a high level of self-awareness, as well as good social communication and comprehension—just what is lacking in children with AS. Lacking social foresight and being so literal and cognitively rigid, a child with AS finds it difficult to perceive why becoming uncomfortable for a brief period of time is worth it for enduring changes. It is usually difficult for children in the spectrum to understand how treatment can make their lives better, or see the value of self-development for its own sake. This is another reason why treatment needs to be explained and framed in language that makes sense to the child or why treatment often winds up having to be imposed, at least initially. Children who can learn to dislike their OCBs—or come to realize that whatever sense of control, tension reduction, or gratification their OCBs provides is just not worth it—would seem to have a much better chance of success. Among those with AS, individuals who learn to value controlling their OCBs for the higher purpose of achieving more ability to connect with themselves as well as with others might have the greatest possibility of making truly meaningful changes in their lives.

A specific concern is the trouble that people with AS have in differentiating affective states, like the level of anxiety or discomfort. Therefore, providing verbal feedback that is useful for conducting ERP, like the SUDS ratings previously described, may be very challenging for them. It is often helpful to create something tangible for them to manipulate, like an actual "discomfort thermometer."

Expected Length of Treatment

Many parents rightly want to know how long treatment of OCBs may be expected to last. Obviously, treatment can be costly in terms of money, time, and emotional strain. There can be long stretches when there is minimal or no progress. Also, so many variables go into making an educated guess about length of treatment that it is artificial, maybe even morally wrong, to answer as if one has a crystal ball or the field is advanced to this state of knowledge. Practically speaking, estimates of treatment duration are based upon mutual agreement about goals. Some parents might prefer a briefer course of treatment focusing on psychoeducation, parent training, and instruction in the basics of OCB treatment. For other parents, the desired treatment is open-ended, trying to make improvements and push the envelope as far as possible. The important thing is for parents and treatment professionals to be on the same page about expected length of treatment and goals. For parents, it is also important to be realistic, since a slower pace of treatment, decreased rates of expected gains, and higher probabilities of periods of plateaus and regression are common in this area.

Setting

What is the best venue to treat OCBs: at home, in a clinician's office, or in a hospital? Parents probably get pretty tired of hearing health professionals answer "It depends," although this is usually the most accurate response. So much depends on the age of the child, the clinical and intellectual profile, the overall family circumstances, symptom severity, what resources are readily available, and so on. There are advantages and disadvantages to each type of setting. The more structured and intensive the setting, the more there is availability for careful observation and the staff necessary for maximizing consistency and also assuring the highest level of safety in the case of trying different kinds or doses of medication. However, this kind of environment is least like the real world that the child and parents have to live in, which raises the question of transferring the results back home. Sadly, the progress that some children with AS can make in controlling their OCBs is hard to reproduce outside of a highly structured placement.

Habituation

As previously noted, OCBs co-occurring with Asperger's tend to elicit less distress and anxiety in children than would be expected in classic OCD. Ironically, this is a negative prognostic factor for improvement. The reasons are twofold: Less distress and anxiety is equated with less motivation for change, and without distress or anxiety there is less opportunity to take advantage of the habituation process. And without habituation, the chance of durable and self-perpetuating neurobiological changes from exposure-based therapies is likely lessened.[114]

Participation in Therapy

It is not surprising that the social difficulties that typify those with Asperger's and OCBs can affect engagement in the process of therapy. Children with this profile are prone either to extremes of disengagement (not relating to the therapist) or, conversely, to disinhibited, impulsive behaviors that interfere with their sessions. In the case of children who compulsively talk about restricted or idiosyncratic topics, therapists can easily be steamrolled, especially if they lack the experience to handle this problem. In the case of children who are withdrawn or guarded, progress can be glacial and quite discouraging to all involved. When a child is angrily resistant, parents may mistakenly interpret this behavior to mean that there is a lack of compatibility with the therapist and may seek out a therapist that the child finds easier to deal with. While there may sometimes be a nonproductive mismatch between child and therapist, often being patient and allowing the two sufficient time to work out their issues or power struggles is the best option. Therapy should ideally not be a popularity contest. Ironically, some therapists who are initially liked best by a child can wind up being the least effective choice in the long run. Additionally, it is important for parents not to allow the child unwarranted control over the therapy, inadvertently reinforce avoidance behaviors, or succumb to their own need to be a hero and "rescue" their child from a practitioner who must eventually challenge the child's behaviors and ideas.

Helping this population use therapy sessions constructively is an art as well as a science. For the therapist, it is important to find the balance between being too didactic, structured, or controlling (all of which risk leading to disengagement or, perhaps, oppositional behaviors) and being too loose, too eager to become the child's "friend" (which risks leading to loss of the purpose and goals of the treatment).

Prognosis for Obsessive-Compulsive Behaviors Occurring in Asperger's Syndrome

What can parents realistically expect regarding the results of appropriate interventions for obsessive-compulsive behaviors, including cognitive behavioral therapy and medication, alone or together, and/or in combination with the other modalities described earlier? As noted, there is a lack of research to guide us in giving a good answer, a situation which is undoubtedly very frustrating to parents, especially given the time, effort, and financial and—not least of all—emotional commitments that are often invested in this process. My clinical experience suggests that, not surprisingly, poor motivation—from the child, the parents, or both—is a major barrier to a good outcome. If we seek some guidance from the available research about OCD, unfortunately what we learn is somewhat discouraging if we want to generalize to the prognosis for OCBs occurring in Asperger's syndrome; children and adolescents with poor insight into their symptoms tend to have the poorest outcomes.[115] Unfortunately, as has been noted, poor insight into their OCBs is commonplace among those with AS.

As painful as it might be for parents to hear, no therapist can meaningfully guarantee to totally eliminate a child's OCBs. Practitioners who make such guarantees are likely either not that experienced in this area or are hungry for business.

The problem is that there are so many variables to consider, including the child's age, the severity and nature of both OCBs and AS, the presence of comorbidities (like depression, tics, or learning disorders), the child's and the parents' motivational levels, the resilience of the parents when coping with setbacks, the availability and expertise of practitioners, and so on. And who is to say in a given case what constitutes improvement? For some parents, anything short of total victory over OCBs is unacceptable; for others, even infinitesimal gains are cause for celebration.

What can be said is this: All elements considered, with the outcome by no means certain, parents must make very hard decisions about the type of treatment, duration of treatment, and when to not consider treatment or to conclude treatment that appears unlikely to help the overall situation. Actually, in some respects, it's not unlike what is gone through with complex medical conditions like cancer. Often, it's helpful to get a variety of opinions on this subject, from members of the treatment team as well as from family members and friends. However, sometimes it all boils down to intangibles, like the parents' gut feeling about how to best meet the needs of their child.

Sharing my experience, when it comes to treating OCBs among those with Asperger's in real-life settings there are always children who seemingly have made exceptional improvement, children who have made some improvement, and children who have made minimal or no gains. Similarly, there are parents who are nothing short of thrilled with their child's progress, as well as parents who have ended therapy expressing bitterness and evidently feeling that they have wasted their time and money. What does this all mean? In a scientific sense, not so much, because in practice the variables are so complex that experiences cannot be evaluated as systematically as they would be in a research lab. What those in the front lines of treatment are often left with are anecdotes and opinions, although hopefully educated ones. For instance, my opinion is that emphasizing the behavioral aspects of therapy over the cognitive aspects tends to be more productive for this population.

My perception, which admittedly reflects the inherent bias of a practitioner, is that there seems to be some relationship between just hanging in there in a course of treatment that is as research based as possible and attaining at least some degree of improvement in OCBs. To me, it makes sense that patience, persistence, and a reasonable plan followed on a regular basis would pay off, just as it usually does in other areas of life. This does not mean staying with the same therapist no matter what; sometimes there is a poor match or the need for a fresh perspective, including obtaining other opinions.

Action for Parents

If treatment has continued for an extended period of time without apparent benefit, ask the relevant practitioner(s) about the prognosis for improvement, given staying the course versus trying a different approach.

Relapse Prevention

This section concerns what happens after an active phase of treatment has resulted in significant gains. As in many conditions, when it comes to obsessive-compulsive behaviors, setbacks (also known as lapses) and relapses (severe regressions to pre-intervention levels of problems) are not only possible, they are virtually inevitable.[116] How to interpret, react to, and cope with these problems and then have the skills to get back on track is an integral part of any intervention plan.

Adopting and sticking to new habits is hard for anyone, but especially for children and parents trying to change OCBs in Asperger's syndrome. In general, regression after a period of improvement is frequently associated with understandable feelings like frustration, discouragement, hopelessness, and anger, along with a tendency for old, unhelpful habits to reemerge. Trying to apportion blame for setbacks is a waste of time and effort. It is far more useful to concentrate on the following:

- Building relapse prevention into the initial intervention plan and understanding the importance of follow-up "booster" sessions. Like diabetes or hypertension, OCBs are chronic and relapse-prone conditions that are wise to monitor on a regular basis.

- Accepting ups and downs as a natural and expected part of the process.

- Becoming aware of situational and emotional setback triggers, which could run the gamut from an unexpected change in a classroom routine to being teased by a peer, and planning how to avoid or deal with them.

- Identifying seemingly unimportant decisions, the little steps that do not appear consequential at first, but over time lead toward relapse (e.g., giving in to a minor OCB "just this one time").

- Understanding that minor life issues do not have to be magnified into major ones.

- Learning to treat, or reframe, a setback as a challenge and learning experience rather than a sure sign of failure.

- Understanding the difference between lapses (temporary, easily modified events) and relapses (full-blown and sustained returns to pretreatment levels of difficulty).

- Knowing about the abstinence violation effect, which is the problem of giving up entirely after a period of improvement is violated by a setback.

- Knowing when it is time to once again step up the level of intervention.

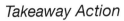

Takeaway Action

By this time, you might be thinking about ways to apply what you have been reading about. Take note of three main points made in this section that you can start to focus on as priorities.

Section IV
Parenting Strategies

Being loving and trying to maintain a sense of normalcy without engaging in denial, appeasement, or any other actions that can keep a child—or themselves—from making progress can be enormously complicated for parents of children with Asperger's syndrome.

Parents of children with AS often feel stuck, uncertain about what the best approach might entail. Frequently, and commonly at first, they may lack accurate information. Some parents may feel that they should be able to address their child's issues alone; however, this feeling may prevent or delay seeking needed professional help, or even accepting needed support of friends and relatives. Parents can become stuck in unwarranted optimism and wishful thinking, too.

If parents in this situation are to become unstuck—that is, to be in the position to assist their children as well as gain some sense of control, even mastery, over their circumstances for their own good—they need to learn the concepts and skills necessary to adapt to their situation for the long run. As part of this process, some may find that many of their preconceptions about how to be an effective and caring parent require significant reshaping.

For parents, being stuck in the world of obsessive-compulsive behaviors means that, on top of everything else, they are dealing with children who might be unable to move easily around their own homes because they are obsessed with making "projects" and exhibit uncontrollable tantrums if their "masterpieces" are touched or moved in even the slightest way. Their sons or daughters may be stuck in a bottomless pit of repetitive discussions about subjects such as superheroes, Greek mythology, or obscure television actors. Perhaps they cannot stop talking about narrow and mundane subjects, like the daily weather report or how long a battery charge might last. Faced with these out-of-the-ordinary problems, commonsense parenting approaches—like explaining, giving choices, waiting until they grow out of it, or tough love—are, unfortunately, all at best ineffective, and at worst detrimental. Even parents with many resources at their disposal often find themselves at a complete loss to understand or cope with their child's OCBs and unable to move forward. And again, if OCBs go unrecognized, are misunderstood, or are ineffectively addressed, risk factors for a worsened prognosis may be increased.

The ultimate hope is that as more parents gain the knowledge and strategies to respond to OCBs, as well as the other difficulties associated with AS that were reviewed in earlier sections, as early and effectively as possible, and develop the wherewithal to obtain and support appropriate treatments, outcomes for children with Asperger's—and their parents and family members—will improve.

Fortunately, we live in an era when past negative mind-sets about improving the lives of children with developmental and neurobiological conditions are being steadily challenged. There are constant and exciting developments in genetic research, medicine, and the behavioral and psychological sciences. Once shunted to the sidelines, many of these children now have far more opportunities to participate in the mainstream. However, there remains plenty of room for further improvement. As adults, how many children with ASDs who have had "accommodations" and "inclusions" still wind up leading marginal and unfulfilling lives? Too many!

Practicing Self-Acceptance

Parents often feel as if they should not have negative feelings, or they experience shame or guilt if they do. This perspective is not realistic or helpful. Minimizing, denying, or "stuffing" one's very understandable emotions is simply not healthy and, in the long run, is very likely to backfire. In fact, habitually suppressing feelings is associated with episodic outbursts of emotions as well as with eventual detachment or, sometimes, even feeling like giving up is the only choice left.

It is totally normal to feel inadequate and experience negative emotions like frustration, anger, anxiety, or sadness when trying to cope with a child whose problems defy resolution, as is often the case with Asperger's. So if parents of a child with AS are feeling overwhelmed, at the end of their rope, or exhausted, they should rest assured that they are not the only ones having these kinds of reactions. Trying to be patient and forgiving of themselves is allowed. No parent, no matter how much they care or how hard they try, can be perfect.

Action for Parents

Take note of whether you have been blaming yourself for factors in your child's life that are beyond your control, or anyone's. If so, it may be helpful to come up with two or three kind and forgiving self-statements on the hour until this self-defeating pattern is significantly decreased.

Making Connections with Other Affected Parents

Parents raising a child who has Asperger's syndrome can feel quite isolated and alone in their struggles. Even though it doesn't directly change their own plight, it nonetheless may comfort them to know that there are many, many parents facing the same kinds of challenges that they are (remember the virtual epidemic of autism spectrum disorders noted earlier in this book). Some of the situations other parents are experiencing may be similar to one's own; some may be quite different. Nevertheless, parents of children with AS usually have at least some of the following in common:

- They love their children and want more than anything for them to grow up happy and healthy.
- They worry about whether they are demonstrating the best parenting

practices and whether they are making the right day-to-day decisions for their child's future.

- Their lives are deeply affected by having a child with special needs in ways that only those in similar situations might comprehend to any extent and in some ways that only they themselves truly understand.

Action for Parents

If you know any parents who are in a situation similar to yours (try to focus on the commonalities rather than the differences), see if you can get together for mutual support and exchanging of information. If you do not know any, consider asking the service providers in your area whether they can facilitate an introduction.

Being Optimistic But Realistic

Even with training, experience, and motivation, clinicians face abundant challenges in treating Asperger's syndrome, and particularly obsessive-compulsive behaviors. The best strategies are often hard to determine and even the most thoughtful approaches don't always produce the desired results in the desired time frame. Often, the reality is that trial and error and persistent hard work are needed to find and implement effective strategies, let alone see meaningful results. It is also common to require involvement of specialists from different disciplines at different times and sometimes as a team. No one practitioner or specialty is likely to have all the answers or skills that are necessary.

As noted earlier, some parents believe that they should be able to meet all of their child's needs on their own, as if they were superhuman, but most inevitably come to find that this is not feasible. Nor can any parent follow the optimal therapeutic approach for their child 100% of the time.

Often, progress for a child with AS must be measured in very modest amounts; there are also some very complicated and severe situations in which, despite the best efforts, gains cannot be made—except in terms of the parents' acceptance level. Yet, on a much more upbeat note, some parents who have patience and realistic goals, seek professional support when needed, and have a long-term commitment to a sensible and well-established intervention process may be rewarded with results that are beyond their expectations; that is to say, their children may become more actualized in their ability to function in life and also happier than they ever dreamed possible.

Coping with Stress

Parenting a child with a multidimensional, chronic developmental and psychological condition is stressful, no matter what. Strain on one's health, work, finances, and relationships is basically inevitable.

One of the keys for parents to adapt as positively as possible to having a child with Asperger's syndrome is to develop expertise in coping. Parents who take good care of themselves and maintain strong relationships with their own support team—whether people they have an intimate bond with or close friends—will likely be in the best position to help a child with special needs. If parents act like martyrs, they are likely needlessly increasing their own suffering, and actually not setting a good example for their child.

Essentially, positive coping means adjusting or adapting constructively to challenge or change; that is, to stress. And stress is anything that necessitates an adjustment. Stress per se is neither inherently positive nor negative; it is what you make of it. For example, winning the lottery can be a negative experience for some people and, for others, the best thing that ever happened to them.

Stress can be decreased by reducing pressure or increasing level of adjustment. At times, there actually are ways to reduce pressure; for example, by moving a child to a school that better fits his or her needs or getting respite assistance. Most of the time, however, the pressures are what they are and the only course available is to increase one's ability to cope.

Certainly, caring about and assisting a child with AS would present a major challenge to anyone. Further, since nothing in life can be expected to stay the same (contrary to the desires of individuals with the conditions being discussed), having good coping skills is necessary. Of course, there are both positive and negative ways of coping. Positive ways of coping include the following:

- Exercise (Even moderate exercise is good for the spirit as well as the body. Regular exercise has been shown to improve general resiliency and reduce mild to moderate levels of depression and anxiety.)[117]

- Meditation, mindfulness (staying focused on one's immediate experiences and environment), and progressive muscle relaxation

- Restructuring your thinking to more accurately reflect reality and to experience less distress

- Accepting the reality of the situation

Among the numerous ways to cope negatively are:

- Losing self-control by overreacting

- Becoming verbally or physically abusive

- Seeking to place blame

- Withdrawing, minimizing or denying that there is a problem

- Engaging in infantilizing and other enabling behaviors

- Ignoring your health by having poor nutrition or sleep habits, abusing legal or illegal substances, or being sedentary

- Focusing on the negative and engaging in self-pity

Action for Parents

Identify strengths that you have shown throughout your life in coping with difficulties. Maybe this will spark an idea or two that can be applied to the challenges of parenting a child with AS.

Developing Self-Efficacy

In psychological terminology, a person's belief that they can accomplish what they set out to do is called self-efficacy. It has been demonstrated many times that just having high self-efficacy in and of itself makes success on most any given task more likely; believing that you can achieve your goals seems to increase the probability that you will engage in the very behaviors required to attain them.[118] Thus, people who believe that they can learn Spanish are more likely to invest the time necessary to master this language. This concept is quite applicable to parents reading this material—if they begin with a high sense of self-efficacy that they can learn to be an effective parent of a child with Asperger's syndrome, they have immediately increased their chances of reaching this goal.

Action for Parents

On a scale from 1 to 10 (highest), mentally rate how strongly you believe that you can learn to effectively parent your child with AS, even when it comes to obsessive-compulsive behaviors. If your rating is 8 or higher, you are starting out with a positive mind-set. If your self-efficacy is below this level, don't be discouraged; see if the next section helps.

Using Pep Talks

If parents don't believe in themselves, they have already decreased their chances of success. One great way to boost self-efficacy is to give yourself a pep talk, which is made up of positive self-statements that indicate belief in you, the intention to keep trying no matter how many obstacles you face, hopefulness about the future, and a commitment to translating good intentions into constructive actions. For an example to follow, it may be helpful to think of a politician, general, coach of a sports team, or religious leader whom you have heard giving an inspiring pep talk. How might being one's own best booster sound? Here's an example:

"It may not be easy and it may not be fair that my child has Asperger's, not to mention obsessive-compulsive behaviors, but I am up to the challenge. My child's difficulties are not anybody's fault, so I'm not going to waste any time feeling sorry for myself, feeling angry or frustrated, or looking for someone or something to blame. Instead, I am going to face each new day with a positive attitude and constructive behaviors. No matter what, I will be here for my child as a loving and caring parent. I will go to bed each night knowing that I have given it my all and with high confidence that I will be able to meet the challenges that tomorrow brings."

Action for Parents

What are you waiting for? Give yourself an inspiring speech. If it's not working for you, try again within a couple of days.

Having a Flexible Attitude

Positive coping is all about being flexible, like going with the flow if there is an unanticipated change in your schedule; isn't this what you'd want your child to do? Rigid attitudes and behaviors in caregivers can not only exacerbate the child's obsessive-compulsive behaviors but also represent another instance that can work against setting a good example. Flexibility is a healthful practice for caregivers who may be uniquely prone to stress-related illnesses (e.g., headaches, stomachaches, backaches, and high blood pressure/cardiovascular disease). Combining flexibility with a good sense of humor; a calm, neutral attitude; reasonable expectations; an appropriate perspective; and a repertoire of positive and adaptive stress-management skills is the best recipe for coping and has the additional benefit of strengthening the foundation for effective intervention strategies.

Action for Parents

Spot a few ways that your parenting style could show some more flexibility. Try these ideas out and see what happens.

Maintaining a Calm Demeanor

The way we express our attitudes and emotions is also reflective of our ability to cope. Raising one's voice, being bitingly sarcastic, avoiding interactions, withholding empathy and love, and showing pity, frustration, or contempt are all unhelpful and ineffective reactions to obsessive-compulsive behaviors. In fact, these sorts of reactions will just create more stress and probably only serve to make OCBs and other issues affecting those with AS worse. Paying too much attention to a child's negative problem behaviors is actually reinforcing and therefore will serve to make these same problem behaviors more likely in the future and also contribute to the child's developing a poor self-image.

A much more effective approach would be maintaining a calm and emotionally neutral demeanor, no matter the circumstances. This, of course, is easier said than done, particularly for those who have high levels of stress in their lives as well as those parents who are reactive, obsessive-compulsive, perfectionistic, or anxious themselves. However, like most behavioral skills, this approach can be learned and become consistent over time with practice.

Action for Parents

Select a day to pretend you are a super-cool and nonreactive character in a movie. Stay in this role no matter what happens during this entire day.

Coping with the Reactions of Others

It can be very upsetting and challenging to parents when their child with

AS does something in public that garners a negative reaction from other people, or even a perceived negative reaction. Following is an example that pertains to what can happen if the child's obsessive-compulsive behaviors are manifested in plain sight:

> A mother and her son are in a mall, and he has a meltdown because they are taking a nonpreferred route, a "wrong" path, back to the parking garage: a fairly common obsessive-compulsive behavior. As her son is screaming and trying to pull her in the direction he wants to go, an older gentleman makes an audible comment to his companion about how parents today just don't know how to control and discipline their kids.

What should parents do if they are in a similar situation? In daily life, anything even a little out of the ordinary—picture a woman with a parrot on her shoulder—is typically going to get attention from other people, so it should be expected that if a child with Asperger's manifests OCBs in a public setting, other people will notice or have demonstrable reactions. Nevertheless, it can be very painful for parents when their beloved child gets stares or actual negative responses from other people for this behavior. When dealing with problematical situations like these, parents' natural impulses can range from wanting to step in and defend their child like a fiercely protective lion to feeling like crawling into a shell out of sheer embarrassment. Often, however, parents just don't know what to do. Experiencing at least a few stressful circumstances like this is probably unavoidable.

Rather than engaging in negative interactions with others who are not being as compassionate as they could be or are being overtly negative about the child's behavior—or the parents' abilities—here are some suggestions to help avoid purposelessly making matters worse, regardless of any sense of justification or emotions:

- Make very sure that looking for an excuse to take out your own frustrations on someone else isn't the real agenda.
- Refrain from "mind-reading" what others are thinking in reference

to your child or you; this can easily lead to jumping to the wrong conclusion.

- Try not to act like the problem doesn't exist; doing that might only result in even more unwanted attention.

- Refrain from guilt-tripping others by excessively explaining the child's "special needs" (which also risks mortifying the child) or being too reactive (e.g., saying something like "What are you looking at? Never saw a child having a tantrum before?").

- Don't lose sight of the overall goals by reverting to being too forceful or threatening unrealistically dire consequences, "when I get you home."

- Predict and prevent: It's always worse to be caught off guard. Parents who make a habit of trying to anticipate what problems might occur and mentally rehearse their healthiest responses have an advantage.

Above all, unless it is an extreme emergency, don't give in and appease OCBs! If there is only one takeaway message parents get from this book, this should be it.

It's understandable how stressful situations like this are, but there is still no reason to swear an oath to keep the child in a bubble, forever avoiding all potentially difficult or embarrassing situations. What can parents do that is more constructive? Again, they can do their best to try to cope effectively. Good coping means maintaining realistic expectations for the child, for themselves, and for others the child comes in contact with (e.g., at school, at family gatherings, or during random daily encounters). Not everyone is going to have a mature, reasonable, nonjudgmental, or caring reaction to OCBs. It's generally best to take the approach of being thankful for those who do and trying to be forgiving and understanding toward those who don't. Otherwise, it is likely that a lot of time and energy will be wasted on senseless conflicts, being resentful, and experiencing shame. Parents who cope effectively with having a child whose social presentation is out of the ordinary often have a well-developed sense of perspective or a good sense of humor that serves not only to help them keep a positive attitude but is also an excellent tool for defusing awkward situations.

Let's revisit the situation from the beginning of this section. Although there is no perfect answer, probably the best thing the mother could do would be to stay calm, keep walking in the "wrong" direction, and say very little, perhaps only a quiet "Sorry" to others who are reacting as if they are truly highly disturbed about what they are witnessing. Once the two get back home, it would be advisable for them to incorporate some practice regarding similar situations into the behavior plan and/or child's subsequent therapy sessions.

Action for Parents

Try to inject some mildly humorous comments when faced with a challenging or awkward situation involving your child's behaviors. Remember the importance of not appearing sarcastic or mocking.

Noticing Thoughts, Feelings, and Behaviors

The four children described below each demonstrate obsessive-compulsive behaviors in the context of Asperger's syndrome.

1. Jacob is a ten-year-old boy with AS and average intelligence. He has been driven to watch jets take off from a certain spot on the roof of one of the airport's parking garages every Saturday at the same time for the last three years. The airport is about forty-five miles from Jacob's home, and he insists that only his mother can drive him. He knows all the planes exactly. As each plane takes off, Jacob mechanically states its model and airline name. At home, he has an enormous number of airplane models in his bedroom; there are so many that they cover much of the floor. He becomes highly agitated if any of these models are moved even slightly, and it has become virtually impossible to clean his room.

2. At the age of eleven, Emily has the typical social issues and confusing emotions of an adolescent with AS. Compounding her problems are rituals involving her head, arms, legs, and other body parts. For example, Emily has to shake her head three times if she has a thought that she believes means she will have bad luck. Bad luck could mean anything from tripping on her own feet to not being allowed to buy a computer game she wants. She engages in these behaviors even in the presence of her peers, which makes it even harder for her to develop relationships with them.

3. Ryan is just seven years old. He was suspected as having AS very early in his life. He has quite a few facial tics and lately has begun repeating the last parts of sentences he hears. He seems to manifest these behaviors more when in a new situation or meeting other people for the first time. He also becomes angry if his parents don't put him to sleep in the same way every night. If they do anything out of sequence, he insists that they start all over again. At times, this behavior has gone on for as long as an hour. Ryan's parents have become increasingly frustrated and helpless; they are at a loss about what to do.

4. Olivia's IQ is in the gifted range. She is ten years old and very serious looking. She can recite dialogue verbatim and mimic the voices and mannerisms of her favorite movie characters, and her parents are already envisioning a Hollywood career for her. Besides watching films, she has minimal interests, and she has no real friends. Her teachers had been suggesting diagnostic evaluations since Olivia was six but had been put off by her parents, who initially believed she was just more mature than other children and that was the primary reason for her lack of peer relationships. She was recently diagnosed with AS.

Action for Parents

Select one of these four children. What might you think or feel if that child were yours? What responses might you have? This brief exercise can help you learn more about yourself if you are a parent of a child with AS and coexisting OCBs.

Maintaining Perspective about Obsessive-Compulsive Behaviors

It cannot be emphasized enough that, once present at a significant level, the obsessive-compulsive behavior affecting a child with Asperger's syndrome is not a "phase" that is likely to go away over time. Forestalling acceptance and delaying appropriate intervention is, in the final analysis, not healthy or fair, to either child or parent. On the other hand, becoming angry, overly critical, reactive, or violent in response to OCBs is unwarranted, extremely counterproductive, or worse. Generally, people do things that upset us, not to upset us. In other words, parents are well advised not to take their child's OCBs as being personally directed at them.

Coping effectively with OCBs requires a healthy dose of this perspective. Doubtless, these behaviors can be annoying and time-consuming. They can derail plans, schedules, sleep, meals, and jobs. Despite all this, it bears repeating that it is extremely important not to interpret OCBs as purposely or maliciously intended. Remember, children did not choose to have these problems any more than did their parents.

Action for Parents

To help balance perspective about the challenges of OCBs, work on finding as many positive aspects of your situation as you can. If you can't think of any, try again each day until you do.

Recognizing That Every Situation Has Unique Aspects

It may be quite helpful for parents of children with Asperger's syndrome to keep several important points in mind:

- Although this book has focused upon concepts that pertain to many children with AS, children are nevertheless unique, and the importance of not overly generalizing from one particular child's situation and experiences to another's cannot be overemphasized. The proper course of action for one child might not be the best one, or might even be detrimental, for a different child.

- All parents of children with obsessive-compulsive behaviors under the umbrella of AS are unique too. They all bring their own expectations as well as their childhood experiences and current situations and feelings—both positive and negative—to the way they believe best to raise their children.

- Asperger's exists in a larger social context. This context includes the availability of resources, existing situations and stressors within a given social environment and family unit, and belief systems about appropriate ways of approaching life problems that vary across cultures and subcultures.

- There is no surefire method, no perfect or single plan, for addressing OCBs, or many of the other complexities of AS. The best one can ever have is a blueprint that is as evidence based and thoughtful as possible.

Despite the individual nature of every child and situation, parents can do quite a lot to develop their ability to understand and address AS. Learning the basic concepts and strategies pertaining to AS can help in the same way that understanding basic concepts and strategies is helpful in basketball or cooking. There is no guarantee of winning in the former or of producing a tasty dish in the latter, but chances of success are likely enhanced.

Takeaway Action

Reflect on three ways that this section helped you clarify the main issues concerning parenting a child with AS, most especially when it comes to the challenge of coping with OCBs.

Section V
Concluding Thoughts

Whether you are a parent, educator, or clinician, before finishing Stuck, take a moment to reflect on your reading experience, focusing especially on any positive changes in your perspective. No matter what your role, increasing your ability to truly understand the complexities of Asperger's syndrome—and of course, obsessive-compulsive behaviors—can make all the difference in supporting the progress of any child or family facing the array of obstacles presented by this condition.

Given the limitations of the available scientific evidence base about this subject, this book unavoidably has many subjective aspects. Although there have been no easy answers or magical solutions, perhaps you now even more acutely recognize the importance of helping a child with AS face challenges, like OCBs, head-on.

Educators or clinicians may use the material in this book to further stimulate their own thinking regarding interventions or research. Parents: Now seems as good a time as any to reassess your child's needs—and not neglect your own. Perhaps you can take to heart that even if your child (or perhaps some family members or friends) cannot truly appreciate the extent of your love and efforts, your own self-endorsement is the most important one of all.

Throughout, this book has emphasized the value of using ideas and strategies that have the best chance of being effective in the long run, particularly at the beginning when they are often the most difficult to implement. Children with AS can often exceed parents' and professionals' best guesses about how much progress is possible for them to attain.

Therefore, maintaining a persistently optimistic attitude despite all the unavoidable ups and downs is highly encouraged.

As recognized at the outset of this book, the future of the diagnosis of Asperger's syndrome is cloudy. But, regardless of any future label, the problems and needs of these children remain unchanged and the more that these children and those who care deeply about their welfare refuse to accept being "stuck" in every way possible, the better.

Takeaway Action for Parents

Consider committing right now to some of the positive changes suggested in this book or others that you came up with as you read along. It might be a good idea to start with the ones that are the most meaningful to you. To further strengthen your resolve, set a date within the next month to review your progress.

Ten Tips for Getting Unstuck

1. Accept children as people who have Asperger's; don't accept maladaptive behaviors, like obsessive-compulsive behaviors, that they have the potential to change.

2. Plan for children with AS to have a wide range of experiences, even if they resist at first. Don't allow them to focus on any one interest or activity to the exclusion of everything else in their lives.

3. Know the difference between a talent that has a real purpose and an OCB.

4. Focus on helping children to function in social settings, not on how they feel about participating at a given moment.

5. Realize that OCBs are not just a phase and are more likely to escalate than decrease without active work on making improvements.

6. Refrain from mocking or being sarcastic. While modeling a gentle sense of humor can be instructional for children with AS and OCBs, sarcasm and mockery are unacceptable and will only compound existing issues.

7. Resist reinforcing symptoms by participating in a child's OCBs.

8. Keep in mind that if it sounds too good to be true, it probably is. Although far from perfect, there is an established scientific evidence base to guide interventions for AS and OCBs.

9. Develop good stress management skills and lead a healthful life. By doing so, parents and other caregivers actually expand their capabilities for assisting a child who needs them. Self-care does not mean selfishness!

10. Remember that it's not a sign of ignorance or incompetence to seek help; quite the opposite. There is always a positive action that can be taken, no matter how small. More often than not, big changes start with lots of little changes in the right direction.

Resources

About Asperger's Syndrome

Websites

American Psychological Association: www.apa.org

Autism Internet Modules: www.autisminternetmodules.org

Autism Research Institute: www.autism.com

Autism Society of America: www.autism-society.org

Autism Speaks: www.autismspeaks.org

Brave Kids: www.ucp.org/about/programs-initiatives/peo/bravekids

CARD (Center for Autism and Related Disorders): www.centerforautism.com

Childnett TV: www.childnett.tv

First Signs: www.firstsigns.org

INSAR (International Society for Autism Research): www.autism-insar.org

NAMI (National Alliance on Mental Illness): www.nami.org

National Institute of Mental Health: www.nimh.nih.gov

National Institutes of Health Clinical Trials: www.clinicaltrials.gov

OAR (Organization for Autism Research): www.researchautism.org

Rethink Autism: www.rethinkautism.com

UM-NSU Center for Autism and Related Disabilities: www.umcard.org

Books

For Adults

Lawson, W. (2003). *Build your own life: A self-help guide for individuals with Asperger's syndrome.* Philadelphia, PA: Jessica Kingsley Publishers.

Newport, J. (2001). *Your life is not a label: A guide to living fully with autism and Asperger's syndrome.* Arlington, TX: Future Horizons, Inc.

Willey, L. H. (1999). *Pretending to be normal: Living with Asperger's syndrome.* Philadelphia, PA: Jessica Kingsley Publishers.

To Explain Social Deficits for Adolescents

Jackson, L. (2002). *Freaks, geeks and Asperger syndrome: A user guide to adolescence.* Philadelphia, PA: Jessica Kingsley Publishers.

Levine, M. (2001). *Jarvis Clutch: Social spy.* Cambridge, MA: EPS School Specialty.

For Children

Faherty, C. (2000). *Asperger's: What does it mean to me?* Arlington, TX: Future Horizons, Inc.

Schnurr, R. G. (1999). *Asperger's huh? A child's perspective.* Gloucester, ON: Anisor Publishing.

Welton, J. (2003). *Can I tell you about Asperger syndrome?* Philadelphia, PA: Jessica Kingsley Publishers.

To Address Social Skills in General

Duke, M., Martin, A., & Nowicki, S. (1996). *Teaching your child the language of social success.* Atlanta, GA: Peachtree Publishers.

Winner, M. G. (2002). *Inside out: What makes a person with social cognitive deficits tick?* Philadelphia, PA: Jessica Kingsley Publishers.

Winner, M. G. (2007). *Thinking about you, thinking about me.* San Jose, CA: Think Social Publishing.

For Parents

Attwood, T. (2008). *The complete guide to Asperger's syndrome.* Philadelphia, PA: Jessica Kingsley Publishers.

Bolick T. (2004). *Asperger syndrome and adolescence: Helping preteens and teens get ready for the real world.* Lions Bay, BC: Fair Winds Press.

Myles, B. S., & Adreon, D. (2001). *Asperger syndrome and adolescence: Practical solutions for school success.* Shawnee Mission, KS: Autism Asperger Publishing Co.

For Teachers

Bolick T. (2004). *Asperger syndrome and adolescence: Helping preteens and teens get ready for the real world.* Lions Bay, BC: Fair Winds Press.

Fein, D., & Dunn, M. A. (2007). *Autism in your classroom: A general educator's guide to students with autism spectrum disorders.* Bethesda, MD: Woodbine House.

Myles, B. S., & Adreon, D. (2001). *Asperger syndrome and adolescence: Practical solutions for school success.* Shawnee Mission, KS: Autism Asperger Publishing Co.

Myles, B. S., Adreon, D., & Gitlitz, D. (2006). *Simple strategies that work! Helpful hints for all educators of students with Asperger syndrome, high-functioning autism, and related disabilities.* Shawnee Mission, KS: Autism Asperger Publishing Co.

Savner, J. L., & Myles, B. S. (2000). *Making visual supports work in the home and community: Strategies for individuals with autism and Asperger syndrome.* Shawnee Mission, KS: Autism Asperger Publishing Co.

About OCD and Related Disorders

Websites

Anxiety Disorders Association of America: www.adaa.org

Association for Behavioral and Cognitive Therapies: www.abct.org

CHADD (Children and Adults with Attention Deficit/Hyperactivity Disorder): www.chadd.org

International OCD Foundation: www.ocfoundation.org

Obsessive Compulsive Anonymous:
www.obsessivecompulsiveanonymous.org

Obsessive Compulsive Information Center:
www.miminc.org/aboutocic.asp

Tourette Syndrome Association, Inc.: www.tsa-usa.org

Trichotillomania Learning Center, Inc.: www.trich.org

Books

Abramowitz, J. S. (2009). *Getting over OCD: A 10-step workbook for taking back your life.* New York, NY: Guilford Press.

Chansky, T. E. (2001). *Freeing your child from obsessive-compulsive disorder.* New York, NY: Three Rivers Press.

Gravitz, H. L. (2004). *Obsessive-compulsive disorder: New help for the family.* Holt, MI: Partners Publishers Group.

Hyman, B., & Dufrene, T. (2008). *Coping with OCD: Practical strategies for living well with obsessive-compulsive disorder.* Oakland, CA: New Harbinger Publications, Inc.

Hyman, B. M., & Pedrick, C. (2005). *The OCD workbook: Your guide to breaking free from obsessive-compulsive disorder* (2nd ed.). Oakland, CA: New Harbinger Publications, Inc.

March, J.S. (2007). *Talking back to OCD: The program that helps kids and teens say "No way" and parents say "Way to go"*. New York, NY: Guilford Press.

March, J. S., & Mulle, K. (1998). *OCD in children and adolescents: A cognitive-behavioral treatment manual*. New York, NY: Guilford Press.

Moritz, E. K. (2011). *Blink, blink, clop, clop: An OCD storybook*. Weston, FL: Weston Press, LLC.

Neziroglu, F., & Yaryura-Tobias, J. (1995). *Over and over again: Understanding obsessive-compulsive disorder* (rev. ed.). San Francisco, CA: Jossey-Bass Publishers.

Penzel, F. (2000). *Obsessive-compulsive disorders: A complete guide to getting well and staying well*. New York, NY: Oxford University Press, Inc.

Acknowledgments

Stuck could not exist in its present form without the support of Dr. E. Katia Moritz, my distinguished clinical and creative partner. She has an extraordinary gift for translating complicated psychological knowledge into practical and humanistic terms. I am very fortunate and grateful for her unwavering generosity in discussing ways to improve the manuscript throughout the writing and publishing process.

Heartfelt appreciation also goes to my colleague Marilyn Cugnetto, Ph.D. Dr. Cugnetto's comments and help with researching this book were invaluable. Amber Hamid very ably assisted her in this effort.

This book's editor was Karen Schader, whose organizational skills and diligence made major contributions to the finished work. Her patience and many helpful suggestions deserve recognition, as well as enormous gratitude. I am similarly indebted to Susan Cohen for her expertise in creating the book's design and layout.

Finally, I want to thank my wife, Carol, not only for her continued kindness and understanding about the demands of my career, but also because she always works so hard to make our life together wonderful.

Notes

Section I:
Understanding Asperger's Syndrome

1. Asperger, H. (1991). "Autistic psychopathy" in childhood. In U. Frith (Trans. and Ed.), *Autism and Asperger syndrome* (pp. 36-92). Cambridge, England: Cambridge University Press. (Original work published in 1944.)

2. Wing, L. (1981). Asperger's syndrome: A clinical account. *Psychological Medicine, 11,* 115-129.

3. American Psychiatric Association. (1994). *Diagnostic and statistical manual of mental disorders* (4th ed.). Washington, DC: Author.

4. Attwood, T. (2003). Frameworks for behavioral interventions. *Child and Adolescent Psychiatric Clinics of North America, 12,* 65-86.

5. Gray, C. A. (1998). Social stories and comic strip conversations with students with Asperger syndrome and high functioning autism. In E. Schopler, G. B. Mesibov, & L. J. Kunce (Eds.), *Asperger syndrome or high-functioning autism?* (pp. 167-198). New York, NY: Plenum Press.

6. Baron-Cohen, S., & Jolliffe, T. (1997). Another advanced test of theory of mind: Evidence from very high functioning adults with autism or Asperger syndrome. *Journal of Child Psychology and Psychiatry, 38,* 813-822; Baron-Cohen, S., O'Riordan, M., Stone, V., Jones, R., & Plaisted, K. (1999). Recognition of faux pas by normally developing children and children with Asperger disorder or high functioning autism. *Journal of Autism and Developmental Disorders, 29,* 407-418.

7. DiLavore, P. C., Lord, C., & Rutter, M. (1995). The pre-linguistic autism diagnostic observation schedule. *Journal of Autism and Developmental Disorders, 25,* 355-379; Lord, C., Rutter, M., & Le Couteur, A. (1994). Autism Diagnostic Interview-Revised: A revised version of a diagnostic interview for caregivers of individuals with possible pervasive developmental disorders. *Journal of Autism and Developmental Disorders, 24,* 659-685.

8. Grandin, T., & Scariano, M. M. (1986). *Emergence: Labeled autistic.* New York, NY: Warner Books, Inc.

9. Wing, L., Gould, J., & Gillberg, C. (2011). Autism spectrum disorders in the DSM-V: Better or worse than the DSM-IV? *Research in Developmental Disabilities, 32,* 768-773.

10. Frazier, T. W., Youngstom, E. A., Speer, L., Embacher, R., Law, P., Constantino, J., Finding, R. L., Hardin, A. Y., & Eng, C. (2012). Validation of proposed DSM-5 criteria for autism spectrum disorders. *Journal of the American Academy of Child and Adolescent Psychiatry, 51*(1), 28-40.

11. American Psychiatric Association. (2000). *Diagnostic and statistical manual of mental disorders* (4th ed., text rev.). Washington, DC: Author.

12. Kaland, N. (2011). Brief report: Should Asperger syndrome be excluded from the forthcoming DSM-V? *Research in Autism Spectrum Disorders, 5,* 984-989.

13. Centers for Disease Control and Prevention. (2007). Prevalence of autism spectrum disorders–autism and developmental disabilities monitoring network, 14 sites, United States, 2002. Report prepared by the US government, ID: 56(SS01); 12-28.

14. Fombonne, E. (2003). Epidemiological surveys of autism and other pervasive developmental disorders: An update. *Journal of Autism and Developmental Disorders, 33,* 365-382; Matson, J. L., & Kozlowski, A. M. (2011). The increasing prevalence of autism spectrum disorders. *Research in Autism Spectrum Disorders, 5,* 418-425.

15. Fombonne, E. (2005). Epidemiology of autistic disorder and other pervasive development disorders. *Journal of Clinical Psychiatry, 66* (suppl. 10), 3-8.

16. Fombonne, E. (1999). The epidemiology of autism: A review. *Psychological Medicine, 29,* 769-786.

17. Mahoney, G., & Perales, F. (2005). The impact of relationship focused intervention on young children with autism spectrum disorders: A comparative study. *Journal of Development and Behavioral Pediatrics, 26,* 77-85; Vismara, L. A., Colombi, C., & Rogers, S. J. (2009). Can one hour per week of therapy lead to lasting changes in young children with autism? *Autism, 13,* 93-115.

18. Fombonne, E. (2005) Epidemiological studies of autism and pervasive developmental disorders. In F. Volkmar (Ed.), *Handbook of autism and pervasive developmental disorders* (3rd ed., pp. 42-69). New York, NY: Wiley & Sons.

19. DeLong, R. G., & Dwyer, J. T. (1988). Correlation of family history with specific autistic subtypes: Asperger's syndrome and bipolar affective disease. *Journal of Autism and Developmental Disorders, 18,* 593-600; Ghaziuddin, M., Ghaziuddin, N., & Greden, J., (2002). Depression in persons with autism: Implications for research and clinical care. *Journal of Autism and Developmental Disorders, 32,* 299-306.

20. Madsen, K. M., Hviid, A., Vestergaard, M., Schendel, D., Wohlfahrt, J., Thorsen, P., et al. (2002). A population-based study of measles, mumps, and rubella vaccination and autism. *The New England Journal of Medicine, 347,* 1477-1482.

21. Rice, C. (2009). Prevalence of autism spectrum disorders: Autism and developmental disabilities monitoring network, United States, 2002. *Surveillance Summaries, 58,* 1-20; Rice, C., Nicholas, J., Baio, J., Pettygrove, S., Lee, L., Van Naarden Barun, K., et al. (2010). Changes in autism spectrum disorder prevalence in 4 areas of the United States. *Disability and Health Journal, 3,* 186-201; Roelfsema, M. T., Hoekstra, R. A., Allison, C., Wheelwright, S., Brayne, C., Matthews, F. E. (2011). Are autism spectrum conditions more prevalent in an information-technology region? A school-based study of three regions in the Netherlands. *Journal of Autism and Developmental Disorders,* DOI 10.1007/s10803-011-1302-1.

22. Baron-Cohen, S. (2006). The hyper-systemizing, assortative mating theory of autism. *Progress in Neuro-Psychopharmacology & Biological Psychiatry, 30,* 865-872.

23. Bertoglio, K., & Hendren, R. L. (2009). New developments in autism. *Psychiatric Clinics of North America, 32,* 1-14; Veenstra-VanderWeele, J., Christian, S. L., & Cook, Jr., E. H. (2004). Autism as a paradigmatic complex genetic disorder. *Annual Review of Genomics and Human Genetics, 5,* 379-405; Klin, A., Lin, D. J., Gorrindo, P., Ramsay, G., & Jones, W. (2009). Two-year-olds with autism orient to non-social contingencies rather than biological motion. *Nature, 459,* 257-263; Mosconi, M. W., Cody-Hazlett, H., Poe, M. D., Gerig, G., Gimpel-Smith, R., & Piven, J. (2009). Longitudinal study of amygdala volume and joint attention in 2-to 4-year-old children with autism. *Archives of General Psychiatry, 66,* 509-516; Wang, K., Zhang, H., Ma, D., Bucan, M., Glessner, J. T., Abrahams, B. S., & Hakonarson, H. (2009). Longitudinal study of amygdala volume associated with autism spectrum disorders. *Nature, 459,* 528-533.

24. Bertoglio, K., & Hendren, R. L. (2009). New developments in autism. *Psychiatric Clinics of North America, 32,* 1-14.

25. Klin, A., Lin, D. J., Gorrindo, P., Ramsay, G., & Jones, W. (2009). Two-year-olds with autism orient to non-social contingencies rather than biological motion. *Nature, 459,* 257-263.

26. Green, J. & Hollander, E. (2010). Autism and oxytocin: New developments in translational approaches to therapeutics. *Neurotherapeutics: The Journal of the American Society for Experimental Therapeutics, 7,* 250-257.

27. Autism Phenome Project. (n.d.). Retrieved December 19, 2011, from www.ucdmc.ucdavis.edu/mindinstitute/research/app/index.html; Rossi, C. C., Van de Water, J., Rogers, S. J., & Amaral, D.G. (2011). Detection of plasma autoantibodies to brain tissue in young children with and without autism spectrum disorders. *Brain, Behavior, and Immunity, 25,* 1123-1135.

28. Sohn, A., & Grayson, C. (2001). Asperger's syndrome: A square peg in a round hole; How to use cognitive-social integration therapy: A 6 hour seminar for professionals and parents. October 19, 2001, Doylestown, PA, Bucks County Intermediate Unit #22.

29. Fombonne, E. (2005); Taylor, B. (2006). Vaccines and the changing epidemiology of autism. *Child: Care, Health and Development, 32,* 511-519.

30. Nydén, A., Niklasson, L., Ståhlberg, O., Anckarsäter, H., Dahlgren-Sandberg, A., Wentz, E., & Råstam, M. (2010). Adults with Asperger syndrome with and without a cognitive profile associated with "nonverbal learning disability": A brief report. *Research in Autism Spectrum Disorders, 44* (4), 612-618; Bishop, D. V. M. (1989). Autism, Asperger's syndrome and semantic-pragmatic disorder: Where are the boundaries? *British Journal of Disorders of Communication, 24,* 107-121.

31. Lord, C., Rutter, M., & Le Couteur, A. (1994). Autism Diagnostic Interview-Revised: A revised version of a diagnostic interview for caregivers of individuals with possible pervasive developmental disorders. *Journal of Autism and Developmental Disorders, 24,* 659-685.

32. Constantino, J. N., & Gruber, C. P. (2005). *Social responsiveness scale.* Los Angeles, CA: Western Psychological Services.

33. DiLavore, P.C., Lord, C., & Rutter, M. (1995). The pre-linguistic autism diagnostic observation schedule. *Journal of Autism and Developmental Disorders, 25,* 355-379.

34. Sparrow, S. S., Cicchetti, D. V., & Balla, D. A. (2005). *Vineland adaptive behavior scales* (2nd ed.). Circle Pines, MN: American Guidance Service.

35. Harrison, P.L., & Oakland, T. (2003). *Adaptive behavior assessment system* (2nd ed.). San Antonio, TX: Harcourt Assessment.

36. Perkins,T., Stokes, M., McGillivray, J., & Bittar, R. (2010). Mirror neuron dysfunction in autism spectrum disorders. Journal of Clinical Neuroscience, 17, 1239-1243

37. Barkley, R.A. (n.d.). The important role of executive function and self-regulation in ADHD. Retrieved December 15, 2011, from www.russellbarkley.org/content/ADHD_EF_and_SR.pdf.

38. American Psychiatric Association. (2000). *Diagnostic and statistical manual of mental disorders* (4th ed., text rev.). Washington, DC: Author.

39. Rapoport, J., Chavez, A., Greenstein, D., Addington, A., & Gogtay, N., (2009). Autism spectrum disorders and childhood-onset schizophrenia: Clinical and biological contributions to a relation revisited. *Journal of the American Academy of Child & Adolescent Psychiatry, 48,* 10-18.

40. Kanne, S. M., & Mazurek, M. O. (2011). Aggression in children and adolescents with ASD: Prevalence and risk factors. *Journal of Autism and Developmental Disorders, 41*(7), 926-937.

41. Mazurek, M. O., Shattuck, P. T., Wagner, M., & Cooper, B. P. (2011). Prevalence of screen-based media use among youths with autism spectrum disorders. *Journal of Autism and Developmental Disorders,* (Epub ahead of print).

42. Fombonne, E. (1999). The epidemiology of autism: A review. *Psychological Medicine, 29,* 769-786; Fombonne, (2005). Epidemiological studies of autism and pervasive developmental disorders. In F. Volkmar (Ed.), *Handbook of autism and pervasive developmental disorders* (3rd ed., pp. 42-69). New York, NY: Wiley & Sons.

43. Attwood, T. (2003). Frameworks for behavioral interventions. *Child and Adolescent Psychiatric Clinics of North America, 12,* 65-86.

44. Wentz Nilsson, E., Gillberg, C., Gillberg, C., & Rastam, M. (1999). Ten year follow-up of adolescent-onset anorexia nervosa: Personality disorders. *Journal of the American Academy of Child and Adolescent Psychiatry, 38,* 1389-1395; Wentz, E., Gillberg, C., Gillberg, I. C., & Rastam, M. (2001). Ten-year follow-up of adolescent-onset anorexia nervosa: Psychiatric disorders and overall functioning scales. *Journal of Child Psychology and Psychiatry and and Allied Disciplines, 42,* 613-622; Wentz, E., Gillberg, I. C., Gillberg, C., & Rastam, M. (2000). Ten-year follow-up of adolescent-onset anorexia nervosa: Physical health and neurodevelopment. *Developmental Medicine and Child Neurology, 42,* 328-333.

45. Attwood, (2003). Frameworks for behavioral interventions. *Child and Adolescent Psychiatric Clinics of North America, 12,* 65-86.

46. Seligman, M. E. P. (2002). *Authentic happiness: Using the new positive psychology to realize your potential for lasting fulfillment.* New York, NY: Free Press/Simon and Schuster.

47. James, I. (2006). *Asperger's syndrome and high achievement: Some very remarkable people.* London: Jessica Kingsley Publishers.

48. Lewis, M. (2010). *The big short: Inside the doomsday machine.* New York, NY: W.W. Norton & Company, Inc.

49. Autism Votes. (n.d.). *Autism speaks state autism insurance reform initiatives.* Retrieved December 19, 2011, from www.autismvotes.org/site/c.frKNI3PCImE/b.3909861/k.B9DF/State_Initiatives.htm.

50. Hartley, S. L., Barker, E. T., Mailick Seltzer, M., Floyd, F., Greenberg, J., Orsmond, G., & Bolt, D. (2010). The relative risk and time of divorce in families of children with an autism spectrum disorder. *Journal of Family Psychology, 24,* 449-457.

51. Newman, L. (2007). Secondary school experiences of students with autism. *National Center for Special Education Research.* Retrieved December 19, 2011, from www.nlts2.org/fact_sheets/nlts2_fact_sheet_2007_04.pdf.

52. Bott, C. L. (2009). *Collaborative consultation: A multicase study of the partnership between private and public special education programs for students with autism.* Dissertation. Rutgers the State University of New Jersey-New Brunswick.

53. Towbin, K. E. (2003). Strategies for pharmacologic treatment of high functioning autism and Asperger syndrome. *Child and Adolescent Psychiatric Clinics of North America, 12,* 23-45; Volkmar, F., Cook Jr., E., Pomeroy, J., Realmuto, G., Tanguay, P., & Work Group on Quality Issues. (1999). Practice parameters for the assessment and treatment of children, adolescents, and adults with autism and other pervasive developmental disorders. *Journal of the American Academy of Child and Adolescent Psychiatry, 38,* 32S-54S.

54. Towbin, (2003). Strategies for pharmacologic treatment of high functioning autism and Asperger syndrome. *Child and Adolescent Psychiatric Clinics of North America, 12,* 23-45.

55. Gray, C. A. (1998) Social stories and comic strip conversations with students with Asperger syndrome and high functioning autism. In E. Schopler, G. B. Mesibov, & L. J. Kunce (Eds.), *Asperger syndrome or high-functioning autism?* (pp. 167-198). New York, NY: Plenum Press.

56. Toth, K., & King, B. H. (2008). Asperger's syndrome: Diagnosis and treatment. *American Journal of Psychiatry, 165,* 958-963; Volkmar et al., (1999).

57. Howlin, P., & Asgharian, A. (1999). The diagnosis of autism and Asperger syndrome: Findings from a survey of 770 families. *Developmental Medicine and Child Neurology, 41,* 834-839.

58. Toth, K., & King, B. H. (2008). Asperger's syndrome: Diagnosis and treatment. *American Journal of Psychiatry, 165,* 958-963; Volkmar et al., (1999).

59. Close, H. A., Li-Ching, L., Kaufman, C. N., & Zimmerman, A. W. (2012). Co-occurring conditions and changes in diagnosis in autism spectrum disorders. *Pediatrics* (online version).

60. Howlin, P. (2000). Outcome in adult life for more able individuals with autism or Asperger syndrome. *Autism, 4,* 63-83.
61. Murrie, D. C., Warren, J. I., Kristiansson, M., & Dietz, P. E. (2002). Asperger's syndrome in forensic settings. *International Journal of Forensic Mental Health, 1,* 59-70.

Section II:
Obsessive-Compulsive Behaviors

62. American Psychiatric Association. (2000). *Diagnostic and statistical manual of mental disorders* (4th ed., text rev.). Washington, DC: Author.

63. Tolin, D. F., Abramowitz, J. S., Brigidi, B. D., & Foa, E. B. (2003). Intolerance of uncertainty in obsessive-compulsive disorder. *Anxiety Disorders, 17,* 233-242.

64. American Psychiatric Association. (2000). *Diagnostic and statistical manual of mental disorders* (4th ed., text rev.). Washington, DC: Author; Ruscio, A. M., Stein, D. J., Chiu, W. T., & Kessler, R. C. (2010). The epidemiology of obsessive-compulsive disorder in the National Comorbidity Survey Replication. *Molecular Psychiatry, 15,* 53-63; Angst, J., Gamma, A., Endrass, J., Goodwin, R., Ajdacic, V., Eich, D., & Rossler, W. (2004). Obsessive-compulsive severity spectrum in the community: Prevalence, comorbidity, and course. *European Archives of Psychiatry and Clinical Neuroscience, 254,* 156-164.

65. March, J. S., & Benton, C. M. (2007). *Talking back to OCD.* New York, NY: Guilford Press.

66. American Psychiatric Association. (2000). *Diagnostic and statistical manual of mental disorders* (4th ed., text rev.). Washington, DC: Author.

67. Hollingsworth, C. E., Tanguay, P. E., Grossman, L., & Pabst, P. (1980). Long-term outcome of obsessive-compulsive disorder in childhood. *Journal of the American Academy of Child and Adolescent Psychiatry, 19,* 134-144; Swedo, S. E., Rapoport, J. L., Leonard, H. L., Lenane, M., & Cheslow, D. (1989). Obsessive compulsive disorders in children and adolescents: Clinical phenomenology of 70 consecutive cases. *Archives of General Psychiatry, 46,* 335-343.

68. Pediatric OCD Treatment Study (POTS). (2004). Cognitive-behavior therapy, sertraline, and their combination for children and adolescents with obsessive-compulsive disorder: The pediatric OCD treatment study (POTS) randomized controlled trial. *Journal of the American Medical Association, 292,* 1969-1976.

69. Foa, E. B., Abramowitz, J. S., Franklin, M. E., & Kozak, M. J. (1999). Feared consequence, fixity of belief, and treatment outcome in patients with obsessive-compulsive disorder. *Behavior Therapy, 30,* 717-724; Garcia, A. M., Sapyta, J. J., Moore, P. S., Freeman, J. B., Franklin, M. E., March, J. S., et al. (2010). Predictors and moderators of treatment outcome in the pediatric obsessive compulsive treatment study (POTS I). *Journal of the American Academy of Child and Adolescent Psychiatry, 49,* 1024-1033; Storch, E. A., Milsom, V. A., Merlo, L. J., Larson, M., Geffken, G. R., Jacob, M. L., et al. (2008). Insight in pediatric obsessive-compulsive disorder: Associations with clinical presentation. *Psychiatry Research, 160,* 212-220.

70. Barrett, P., Healy-Farrell, L., & March, J. S. (2004). Cognitive-behavioral family treatment of childhood obsessive-compulsive disorder: A controlled trial. *Journal of the American Academy of Child and Adolescent Psychiatry, 43,* 46-62; Barrett, P. M., Farrell, L., Pina, A. A., Peris, T. S., & Piacentini, J. (2008). Evidence-based psychosocial treatments for child and adolescent obsessive-compulsive disorder. *Journal of Clinical Child and Adolescent Psychology, 37,* 131-155; Storch, E. A., Geffken, G. R., Merlo, L. J., Mann, G., Duke, D., Munson, M., et al. (2007). Family-based cognitive-behavioral therapy for pediatric obsessive-compulsive disorder: Comparison of intensive and weekly approaches. *Journal of the American Academy of Child and Adolescent Psychiatry, 46,* 468-478.

71. Micali, N., Hilton, K., Natatani, E., Heyman, I., Turner, C., & Mataix-Cols, D. (2011). Is childhood OCD a risk factor for eating disorders later in life? A longitudinal study. *Psychological Medicine, 41*(12), 2507-2513.

72. American Psychiatric Association. (2000). *Diagnostic and statistical manual of mental disorders* (4th ed., text rev.). Washington, DC: Author.

73. Dar, R., Kahn, D.T., & Carmeli, R. (2011). The relationship between sensory processing, childhood rituals and obsessive-compulsive symptoms. *Journal of behavior therapy and experimental psychiatry, 43*(1), 679-684.

74. American Psychiatric Association. (2000). *Diagnostic and statistical manual of mental disorders* (4th ed., text rev.). Washington, DC: Author.

75. Swedo, S. E., Rapoport, J. L., Leonard, H. L., Lenane, M., & Cheslow, D. (1989). Obsessive compulsive disorders in children and adolescents: Clinical phenomenology of 70 consecutive cases. *Archives of General Psychiatry, 46,* 335-343; Martino, D., Defazio, G., & Giovannoni, G. (2009). The PANDAS subgroup of tic disorders and childhood-onset

obsessive-compulsive disorder. *Journal of Psychosomatic Research, 67,* 547-557; Roan, S. (2011, December 9). Childhood disorder bolsters research on infection link. *Los Angeles Times.*

76. Singer, H. S., Gilbert, D. L., Wolf, D. S., Mink, J. W., & Kurlan, R. (December 2011). Moving from PANDAS to CANS. *The Journal of Pediatrics (online version).*

77. Scahill, L., Riddle, M. A., McSwiggin-Hardin, M., Ort, S. I., King, R. A., Goodman, W. K., et al. (1997). Children's Yale-Brown Obsessive Compulsive Scale: Reliability and validity. *Journal of the American Academy of Child and Adolescent Psychiatry, 36,* 844-852; White, S. W., Oswald, D., Ollendick, T., & Scahill, L. (2009). Anxiety in children and adolescents with autism spectrum disorders. *Clinical Psychology Review, 29,* 216-229.

78. Church, C., Alisanski, S., & Amanullah, S. (2000). The social, behavioral, and academic experiences of children with Asperger syndrome. *Focus on Autism and Other Developmental Disabilities, 15,* 12-20; Ghaziuddin, M., Weidmer-Mikhail, E., & Ghaziuddin, N. (1998). Comorbidity of Asperger syndrome: A preliminary report. *Journal of Intellectual Disability Research, 42,* 279-283.

79. Attwood, T. (2003). Frameworks for behavioral interventions. *Child and Adolescent Psychiatric Clinics of North America, 12,* 65-86; Attwood, T. (2004). Cognitive behavior therapy for children and adults with Asperger's syndrome. *Behaviour Change, 21,* 147-161; Green, J., Gilchrist, A., Burton, D., & Cox, A. (2000). Social and psychiatric functioning in adolescents with Asperger disorder compared with conduct disorder. *Journal of Autism and Developmental Disorders, 30,* 279-293; Kim, J. A., Szatmari, E., Bryson, S. E., Streiner, D. L., & Wilson, E J. (2000). The prevalence of anxiety and mood problems among children with autism and Asperger syndrome. *Autism, 4,* 117-132; White, S. W., Oswald, D., Ollendick, T., & Scahill, L. (2009). Anxiety in children and adolescents with autism spectrum disorders. *Clinical Psychology Review, 29,* 216-229.

80. Mansueto, C. S. & Keuler, D. J. (2005). Tic or compulsion?: It's Tourettic OCD. *Behavior Modification, 29,* 784-799.

81. Baron-Cohen, S., Scahill, V. L., Izaguirre, J., Hornsey, H., & Robertson, M. M. (1999). The prevalence of Gilles de la Tourette syndrome in children and adolescents with autism: A large-scale study. *Psychological Medicine, 29,* 1151-1159.

82. American Psychiatric Association. (2000). *Diagnostic and statistical manual of mental disorders* (4th ed., text rev.). Washington, DC: Author.

83. Swain, J. E., Scahill, L., Lombroso, P. J., King, R. A., & Leckman, J. F. (2007). Tourette syndrome and tic disorders: A decade of progress. *Journal of the American Academy of Child and Adolescent Psychiatry, 46,* 947-968.

84. Chang, S. W., Piacentini, J., & Walkup, J. T. (2007). Behavioral treatment of Tourette syndrome: Past, present, and future. *Clinical Psychology: Science and Practice, 14,* 268-273; Cook, C. R., & Blacher, J. (2007). Evidence-based psychosocial treatments for tic disorders. *Clinical Psychology: Science and Practice, 41,* 252-267; Swain, (2007).

85. Church, C., Alisanski, S., & Amanullah, S. (2000). The social, behavioral, and academic experiences of children with Asperger syndrome. *Focus on Autism and Other Developmental Disabilities, 15,* 12-20; Ghaziuddin, M., Weidmer-Mikhail, E., & Ghaziuddin, N. (1998). Comorbidity of Asperger syndrome: A preliminary report. *Journal of Intellectual Disability Research, 42,* 279-283.

86. American Psychiatric Association. (2000). *Diagnostic and statistical manual of mental disorders* (4th ed., text rev.). Washington, DC: Author; Potenza, M. N., Koran, L. M., & Pallanti, S. (2009). The relationship between impulse-control disorders and obsessive-compulsive disorder: A current understanding and future research directions. *Psychiatry Research, 170,* 22-31.

Section III:
Treating Obsessive-Compulsive Behaviors in Children with Asperger's Syndrome

87. Prochaska, J. O., & Prochaska, J. M. (1999). Why don't continents move? Why don't people change? *Journal of Psychotherapy Integration, 9,* 83-102.

88. Scahill, L., Riddle, M. A., McSwiggin-Hardin, M., Ort, S. I., King, R. A., Goodman, W. K., et al. (1997). Children's Yale-Brown Obsessive Compulsive Scale: Reliability and validity. *Journal of the American Academy of Child and Adolescent Psychiatry, 36,* 844-852.

89. Cooper, J. (1970). The Leyton Obsessional Inventory. *Psychological Medicine, 1,* 48-64.

90. O'Riordan, M., Plaisted, K., Driver, J., & Baron-Cohen, S. (2001). Superior visual search in autism. *Journal of Experimental Psychology: Human Perception and Performance, 27,* 719-730.

91. Hay, Philipa J., Sachdev, P. S., Cumming, S., Smith, J. S., et al. (1993). Treatment of obsessive-compulsive disorder by psychosurgery. *Acta Psychiatrica Scandinavica, 87*(3), 197-207.

92. Lipsman, N., Neimat, J. & Lozano, A. M. (2007). Deep brain stimulation for treatment-refractory obsessive-compulsive disorder. *Neurosurgery, 61*, 1-11.

93. Abramowitz, J. S. (1997). Effectiveness of psychological and pharmacological treatments for obsessive-compulsive disorder: A quantitative review. *Journal of Consulting and Clinical Psychology, 65*, 44-52; Abramowitz, J. S., Franklin, M. E., & Foa, E. B. (2002). Empirical status of cognitive-behavioral therapy for obsessive-compulsive disorder: A meta-analytic review. *Romanian Journal of Cognitive and Behavioral Psychotherapies, 2*, 89-104; Abramowitz, J. S., Whiteside, S. P., & Deacon, B. J. (2005). The effectiveness of treatment for pediatric obsessive-compulsive disorder: A meta-analysis. *Behavior Therapy, 36*, 55-63; Freeman, J. B., Choate-Summers, M .L., Moore, P. S., Garcia, A. M., Sapyta, J. J., Leonard, H. L., et al. (2007). Cognitive behavioral treatment for young children with obsessive-compulsive disorder. *Biological Psychiatry, 61*, 337-343; Pediatric OCD Treatment Study (POTS). (2004). Cognitive-behavior therapy, sertraline, and their combination for children and adolescents with obsessive-compulsive disorder: The pediatric OCD treatment study (POTS) randomized controlled trial. *Journal of the American Medical Association, 292*, 1969-1976; Watson, H.J., & Rees, C.S. (2008). Meta-analysis of randomized, controlled treatment trials for pediatric obsessive-compulsive disorder. *Journal of Child Psychology and Psychiatry, 49*, 489-498.

94. Ritchey, M., Dolcos, F., Eddington, K. M., Strauman, T. J., & Cabeza, R. (2011). Neural correlates of emotional processing in depression: Changes with cognitive behavioral therapy and predictors of treatment response. *Journal of Psychiatric Research, 45*, 577-587; Jockers-Scherübl, M. C., Zubraegel, D., Baer, T., Linden, M., Danker-Hopfe, H., Schulte-Herbrüggen, O., et al. (2007). Nerve growth factor serum concentrations rise after successful cognitive-behavioural therapy of generalized anxiety disorder. *Progress in Neuro-Psychopharmacology & Biological Psychiatry, 31*, 200-204; Saxena, S., Gorbis, E., O'Neill, J., Baker, S. K., Mandelkern, M. A., Maidment, K. M., et al. (2009). Rapid effects of brief intensive cognitive-behavioral therapy on brain glucose metabolism in obsessive-compulsive disorder. *Molecular Psychiatry, 14*, 197-205; Brody, A. L., Saxena, S., Schwartz, J. M., Stoessel, P. W., Maidment, K., Phelps, M. E., et al. (1998). FDG-PET predictors of response to behavioral therapy versus pharmacotherapy in obsessive-

compulsive disorder. *Psychiatry Research: Neuroimaging, 84,* 1-6; Schwartz, J. M., Stoessel, P. W., Baxter Jr., L. R., Martin, K. M., & Phelps, M. E. (1996). Systematic changes in cerebral glucose metabolic rate after successful behavior modification treatment of obsessive-compulsive disorder. *Archives of General Psychiatry, 53,* 109-113; O'Neill, J., Piacentini, J. C., Chang, S., Levitt, J. G., Rozenman, M., Bergman, L., et al. (2012). MRSI correlates of cognitive-behavioral therapy in pediatric obsessive-compulsive disorder. *Progress in Neuro-Psychopharmacology & Biological Psychiatry, 36,* 161-168.

95. Twohig, M. P. (2009). The application of acceptance and commitment therapy to obsessive-compulsive disorder. *Cognitive and Behavioral Practice, 16,* 18-28.

96. Miller, W. R. (2006). Motivational factors in addictive behaviors. In W. R. Miller & K. M. Carroll (Eds.), *Rethinking substance abuse: What the science shows, and what we should do about it* (pp. 143-150). New York: Guilford Press; Miller, W. R., & Rollnick, S. (2002). *Motivational Interviewing* (2nd ed.). New York: Guilford Press.

97. Beck, J. S. (2011). *Cognitive therapy: Basics and beyond,* (2nd ed.). New York, NY: Guilford Press.

98. Salkovskis, P. M. (1985). Obsessional-compulsive problems: A cognitive behavioural analysis. *Behaviour Research and Therapy, 23,* 571-583; Emmelkamp, P. M. G., van der Helm, M. B. L., van Zanten, B. L., & Ploch, G. (1980). Treatment of obsessive-compulsive patients: The contribution of self-instructional training to the effectiveness of exposure. *Behaviour Research and Therapy, 18,* 61-66; Wilhelm, S., Steketee, G., Reilly-Harrington, N. A., Deckersbach, T., Buhlmann, U., & Baer, L. (2005). Effectiveness of cognitive therapy for obsessive-compulsive disorder: An open trial. *Journal of Cognitive Psychotherapy: An International Quarterly, 19,* 173-179.

99. Obsessive Compulsive Cognitions Working Group. (1997). Cognitive assessment of obsessive-compulsive disorder. *Behaviour Research and Therapy, 35,* 667-681.

100. Wilhelm, S., & Steketee, G. S. (2006). *Cognitive therapy for obsessive-compulsive disorder: A guide for professionals.* Oakland, CA: New Harbinger Publications, Inc.

101. Ellis, A. (1994). Rational emotive behavior therapy approaches to obsessive-compulsive disorder. *Journal of Rational-Emotive and Cognitive-Behavior Therapy, 12,* 121-141.

102. Church, C., Alisanski, S., & Amanullah, S. (2000). The social, behavioral, and academic experiences of children with Asperger syndrome. *Focus on Autism and Other Developmental Disabilities, 15,* 12-20; Ghaziuddin, M., Weidmer-Mikhail, E., & Ghaziuddin, N.

(1998). Comorbidity of Asperger syndrome: A preliminary report. *Journal of Intellectual Disability Research, 42,* 279-283.

103. Abramowitz, J. S. (1997). Effectiveness of psychological and pharmacological treatments for obsessive-compulsive disorder: A quantitative review. *Journal of Consulting and Clinical Psychology, 65,* 44-52; Abramowitz, J. S., Franklin, M. E., & Foa, E. B. (2002). Empirical status of cognitive-behavioral therapy for obsessive-compulsive disorder: A meta-analytic review. *Romanian Journal of Cognitive and Behavioral Psychotherapies, 2,* 89-104; Abramowitz, J. S., Whiteside, S. P., & Deacon, B. J. (2005). The effectiveness of treatment for pediatric obsessive-compulsive disorder: A meta-analysis. *Behavior Therapy, 36,* 55-63; Freeman, J. B., Choate-Summers, M. L., Moore, P. S., Garcia, A. M., Sapyta, J. J., Leonard, H. L., et al. (2007). Cognitive behavioral treatment for young children with obsessive-compulsive disorder. *Biological Psychiatry, 61,* 337-343; Pediatric OCD Treatment Study (POTS). (2004). Cognitive-behavior therapy, sertraline, and their combination for children and adolescents with obsessive-compulsive disorder: The pediatric OCD treatment study (POTS) randomized controlled trial. *Journal of the American Medical Association, 292,* 1969-1976; Watson, H. J., & Rees, C. S. (2008). Meta-analysis of randomized, controlled treatment trials for pediatric obsessive-compulsive disorder. *Journal of Child Psychology and Psychiatry, 49,* 489-498.

104. Foa, E. B., & Kozak, M. (1986). Emotional processing of fear: Exposure to corrective information. *Psychological Bulletin, 99,* 20-35.

105. Azrin, N. H., & Nunn, R. G. (1973). Habit reversal: A method of eliminating nervous habits and tics. *Behaviour Research and Therapy, 11,* 619-628; Woods, D. W., Piacentini, J. C., Chang, S. W., Deckersbach, T., Ginsburg, G. S., Peterson, A. L., et al. (2008). Managing Tourette syndrome: A behavioral intervention for children and adults-therapist guide. New York, NY: Oxford University Press.

106. White, S. W., Koenig, K., & Scahill, L. (2007). Social skills development intervention in children with autism spectrum disorders: A review of the intervention research. *Journal of Autism and Developmental Disorders, 37,* 1858-1868.

107. Pawlow, L. A., & Jones, G. E. (2002). The impact of abbreviated progressive muscle relaxation on salivary cortisol. *Biological Psychology, 60,* 1-16.

108. Moritz, E. K., & Jablonsky, J. (1998). *Blink, blink, clop, clop: Why do we do things we can't stop? An OCD storybook.* Plainview, NY: Childswork/Childsplay; Moritz, E. K. (2011). *Blink, blink, clop, clop: An OCD storybook.* Weston, FL: Weston Press, LLC.

109. March, J., Frances, A., Carpenter, D., & Kahn, D. (1997). The expert consensus guideline series: Treatment of obsessive compulsive disorder. *Journal of Clinical Psychiatry, 58* (Supplement 4); American Academy of Child and Adolescent Psychiatry. (1998). Practice parameters for the use assessments and treatment of children and adolescents with obsessive-compulsive disorder. *Journal of the American Academy of Child and Adolescent Psychiatry, 37,* 27S-45S; Rasmussen, S. A., & Eisen, J. L. (1997). Treatment strategies for chronic and refractory obsessive-compulsive disorder. *Journal of Clinical Psychiatry, 58,* 9-13; Greist, J. H., Jefferson, J. W., Koback, K. A., Katzelnick, D. J., & Serlin, R. C. (1995). Efficacy and tolerability of serotonin transport inhibitors in obsessive compulsive disorder: A meta-analysis. *Archives of General Psychiatry, 52,* 53-60; Pallanti, S., Hollander, E., Bienstock, C., et al. (2002). Treatment non-response in OCD: Methodological issues and operational definitions. *International Journal of Neuropsychopharmacology, 5,* 181-91; Murphy, T. (2009). *Medical treatment of OCD.* Presentation at the OCF Behavior Therapy Institute, St. Petersburg, FL; Storch, E. A., & Merlo, L. J. (2006). Obsessive-compulsive disorder: Strategies for using CBT and pharmacotherapy. *The Journal of Family Practice, 55,* 329-333; Denys, D. (2006). Pharmacotherapy of obsessive-compulsive disorder and obsessive-compulsive spectrum disorders. *Psychiatric Clinics of North America, 29,* 553-584.

110. March, J., Frances, A., Carpenter, D., & Kahn, D. (1997). The expert consensus guideline series: Treatment of obsessive compulsive disorder. *Journal of Clinical Psychiatry, 58* (Supplement 4).

111. Bandelow, B., Zohar, J., Hollander, E., Kasper, S., Moller, H., & WFSBP Task Force on Treatment Guidelines for Anxiety, Obsessive-Compulsive, Post-Traumatic Stress Disorders. (2008). World Federation of Societies of Biological Psychiatry (WFSBP) guidelines for the pharmacological treatment of anxiety, obsessive-compulsive, and post-traumatic stress disorders-first revision. *World Journal of Biological Psychiatry, 9,* 248-312; Denys, D. (2006). Pharmacotherapy of obsessive-compulsive disorder and obsessive-compulsive spectrum disorders. *Psychiatric Clinics of North America, 29,* 553-584; Murphy, T. (2009). *Medical treatment of OCD.* Presentation at the OCF Behavior Therapy Institute, St. Petersburg, FL.

112. Chalfant, A. M., Rapee, R., & Carroll, L. (2007). Treating anxiety disorders in children with high functioning autism spectrum disorders: A controlled trial. *Journal of Autism and Developmental Disorders, 39,* 1842-1857; Hare, D. J. (1997). The use of cognitive-behavioral therapy with people with Asperger syndrome: A case study. *Autism, 1,*

215-225; Lord, C. (1995). Treatment of a high-functioning adolescent with autism: A cognitive-behavioral approach. In M. A. Reinecke & F. M. Dattilio (Eds.), *Cognitive therapy with children and adolescents: A casebook for clinical practice* (pp. 394-404). New York, NY: Guilford Press; Sofronoff, K., Attwood, T., & Hinton, S. (2005). A randomized controlled trial of a CBT intervention for anxiety in children with Asperger syndrome. *Journal of Child Psychology and Psychiatry, 46* (11), 1152-1160.

113. Reaven, J. & Hepburn, S. (2003). Cognitive-behavioral treatment of obsessive-compulsive disorder in a child with Asperger syndrome: A case report. *Autism, 7* (2), 145-164.

114. Foa, E. B., & Kozak, M. (1986). Emotional processing of fear: Exposure to corrective information. *Psychological Bulletin, 99,* 20-35.

115. Foa, E. B., Abramowitz, J. S., Franklin, M. E., & Kozak, M. J. (1999). Feared consequence, fixity of belief, and treatment outcome in patients with obsessive-compulsive disorder. *Behavior Therapy, 30,* 717-724; Garcia, A. M., Sapyta, J. J., Moore, P. S., Freeman, J. B., Franklin, M. E., March, J. S., et al. (2010). Predictors and moderators of treatment outcome in the pediatric obsessive compulsive treatment study (POTS I). *Journal of the American Academy of Child and Adolescent Psychiatry, 49,* 1024-1033; Storch, E. A., Milsom, V. A., Merlo, L. J., Larson, M., Geffken, G. R., Jacob, M. L., et al. (2008). Insight in pediatric obsessive-compulsive disorder: Associations with clinical presentation. *Psychiatry Research, 160,* 212-220.

116. Hiss, H., Foa, E. B., & Kozak, M. J. (1994). A relapse prevention program for obsessive-compulsive disorder. *Journal of Consulting and Clinical Psychology, 62,* 801-808.

Section IV:
Parenting Strategies

117. Blumenthal, J. A., Babyak, M. A., Doraiswamy, P. M., Watkins, L., Hoffman, B. M., Barbour, K. A., et al. (2007). Exercise and pharmacotherapy in the treatment of major depressive disorder. *Psychosomatic Medicine, 69,* 587-596.

118. Bandura, A. (1997). *Self-efficacy: The exercise of control.* New York, NY: Freeman.

Made in the USA
·Lexington, KY
10 November 2012